FOOTBALL EXTREME

D1477755

Rob Crossan is a freelance travel, sport and lifestyle journalist whose work appears regularly in *Conde Nast Traveller*, the *Sunday Times Travel* magazine, *CNN Traveller*, the *Financial Times Weekend* magazine, the *Daily Express*, the *Sunday Express*, *Shortlist* and *Time Out* among others. He supports Wrexham FC and lives in Stockwell, South London. This is his first book.

FOOTBALL EXTREME

The craziest, funniest and most bizarre
facts from the world of football

ROB CROSSAN

JOHN BLAKE

Published by John Blake Publishing Ltd,
3 Bramber Court, 2 Bramber Road,
London W14 9PB, England

www.johnblakepublishing.co.uk

www.facebook.com/Johnblakepub **facebook**
twitter.com/johnblakepub **twitter**

First published in paperback in 2011

ISBN: 978-1-84358-318-9

British Library Cataloguing-in-Publication Data:

A catalogue record for this book is available from the British Library.

Design by www.envydesign.co.uk

Printed and bound in Great Britain by CPI Antony Rowe,
Chippenham and Eastbourne

1 3 5 7 9 10 8 6 4 2

Papers used by John Blake Publishing are natural, recyclable products
made from wood grown in sustainable forests. The manufacturing processes
conform to the environmental regulations of the country of origin.

Every attempt has been made to contact the relevant copyright-holders,
but some were unobtainable. We would be grateful if the
appropriate people could contact us.

This book is for my sister.

CONTENTS

Foreword by Chris Kamara   x
Acknowledgements   xi
Introduction   xiii
Extreme FA Cup   1
Extreme Goals   6
Extreme Goals II   10
Extreme Old Age   14
Extreme Cup Replay   18
Extreme Absenteeism   23
Extreme Goalscoring   27
Extreme Culture Shock   31
Extreme Downfall   36
Extremely Strange Stands   41
Extreme Great Escape   45

Extreme Cup Shock – Scotland 49

Extremely Bad Season 53

Extreme Fouls 57

Extremely Bad Transfers 62

Extremely Short England Careers 67

Extremely Bad Predictions 71

Extreme Gobbledygook 76

Extreme Greediness 81

Extreme Match Fixing 85

Extremely Useless Cup Competition 90

Extremely Long Wait 97

Extreme England Thrashing 100

Extremely Bad Misses 105

Extremely Bad Goalkeeping 109

Extreme Expulsion 116

Extremely Brief Managerial Careers 125

Extreme Bad Luck 130

Extreme Mis–Match 135

Extreme Smallness 139

Extremely Bad Matches 143

Extreme Sexism 147

Extreme Refereeing 151

Extreme Magnanimity 155

Extremely Small League 159

Extreme Goals by Inanimate Objects 162

Extreme Cup Shock – England 166

Extremely Large Crowds   171
Extremely Cold Weather   175
Extremely Bad Football Songs   179
Extreme Fatness   183
Extreme Personal Favourite   187

FOREWORD BY CHRIS 'KAMMY' KAMMARA

We've all heard the old Greavsie cliché, 'It's a funny old game', but even I was a bit surprised on reading this book to find out just how many bizarre and peculiar stories there are from the world of British football. Every Saturday I have the honour of travelling around Premiership games watching events unfold but I'm sad to say that, even in my experience, I've yet to see a 20–0 win or a triple hat-trick by one player in a single match – both stories that Rob has uncovered in this wonderful book.

Of course, Jeff Stelling will tell you that maybe things like that *did* happen – but I managed to miss them. 'Red card? I must have missed that, Jeff...!' There's plenty I could say about Jeff too, as it happens, but as this is a family publication I'll leave it for now...

Anyway, this is the perfect book to get stuck into should you find yourself in the middle of a 0-0 bore draw – and it's not a bad book to ponder should you ever have concerns that your team is cursed or just simply dreadful. As you'll see as you make your way through these pages, there's always been a group of supporters who have had it worse than you.

Enjoy the book – 'It's unbelievable, Jeff!'

Chris Kamara

ACKNOWLEDGEMENTS

Huge thanks must go to all of the fanzine editors, message board scribers, online bloggers and football club archivists who have given so much of their time for nothing to help me with this book you're reading. There's far too many to thank here but you know who you are.

Huge thanks also to the local newspapers including the *Oxford Mail* and the *Rochdale Observer*, which have been of so much assistance in digging into their musty back issues for ancient match reports.

Thanks to Allie Collins at John Blake for all her helpful guidance through the writing of this book and, lastly, eternal thanks must go to Gordon Glyn Jones and Eoin and Damien McSorley. Without their help, my pipe dream of being able to make a living from writing about football and travel would have remained exactly that.

INTRODUCTION

George Best, Pelé, David Beckham… none of these people need any more medals, garlands and praise bestowed upon them, and you won't find many mentions of them, or any of the other famous footballing greats, in the following pages.

Rather, this is a book dedicated to the unsung heroes of the game who, in their own myriad ways, have earned a small but special place in football fans' hearts as being part of or culpable for some of the most extreme moments in football history.

Some of them will be familiar to you already, some you will never have heard of before. For me, however, the true spirit of the game doesn't lie with watching endless YouTube clips of the Brazilian 1970 World Cup side. It lies with wondering just who the couple of hundred people were who turned up at Stirling Albion on an ordinary Saturday in December 1984 and ended up witnessing the biggest thrashing in British senior football in the 20th century. Are they still celebrating now? Are they aware of their unique place in history? Were the pies any good that day?

We can't ever know any of these things with certainty, but it's moments like this which provide football with its soul in all its eccentric, obsessive glory – far more than yet another Champions League penalty shoot-out or lucrative multi-million-pound shirt sponsorship deal.

I've always dreamed of being a spectator at an 'extreme' football moment, like the ones you'll read about in the following pages. The closest I have come was in 1992 when, as a typically gauche and callow 12-year-old I was at the Racecourse Ground to watch my team, Wrexham, beat Arsenal 2-1 in the FA Cup third round – one of the biggest cup shocks of all time.

Sadly, this moment doesn't make it into the hallowed pages of *Football Extreme* as the story is just a little too well-known. So instead, this book is full of stories of characters like the Torquay manager who was boss for all of ten minutes – the shortest managerial reign in British football history – or the non-league football coach who guided his team to the FA Cup fifth round by forcing them to drink something that he called 'speed oil'.

Many of the people featured herein will be proud of their small place in football history. Many will be utterly ashamed. Either way, it is these extreme moments, full of idiosyncrasy, farce, hubris and genius that make football the beautiful game it is. So next time you're enjoying an afternoon in your local pub watching Gerrard or Rooney in action on the big screen, spare a thought for those lower down the footballing pyramid. Perhaps you could even make more of a point of taking a closer interest in what goes on away from the tabloid back pages. For here lies football in all its strangest, most alluring and often completely bizarre glory.

Rob Crossan, London, 2011

EXTREME FA CUP

How Blyth Spartans had the most extreme Cup run of any non-league side in modern times

They tell you that the 'magic of the FA Cup' occurs in at least one match every year. The truth is, of course, that barring the odd shock result, the world's oldest cup competition is more or less always won in the end by the top teams. An incredible 35 years have passed since a team from outside the First Division/Premier League has won the thing.

DID YOU KNOW?

Manchester United hold the record for the most FA Cup wins. They have lifted the trophy 11 times – in 1909, 1948, 1963, 1977, 1983, 1985, 1990, 1994, 1996, 1999 and 2004.

However, a club in the Northern League, buried deep in the north east of England and playing in incongruous green–and–white stripes came closer than anyone has come in modern times to actually taking the trophy away from the big boys, thanks to their incredible run in the FA Cup of 1977/78.

All the non-league clichés were in place. A ramshackle stadium, noisy local support and a manager in Jackie Marks who claimed to have invented a special drink called 'speed oil' which the players were instructed to imbibe before games. There was clearly something in the water. Blyth Spartans had already disposed of four local sides in the early stages of the competition before beating Burscough in the first round proper and claiming their first league scalp, Chesterfield, in the second round.

Croft Park was the home to the easiest of third round draws, against Enfield. The brilliantly-named Alan

Shoulder scored the only goal of the game to see Blyth through to their first really big challenge – a trip to Stoke City.

At that time the Potteries side had a young Garth Crooks and Howard Kendall in their ranks and had only recently been relegated from the top flight. Blyth took the lead, but two quick Stoke goals after half-time appeared to spell the end for the non-league outfit. They'd already played an incredible eight matches to get this far – surely their players couldn't possibly have the strength and stamina to turn the game around?

Then, the magic appeared. A free kick followed by a tap-in by Steve Carney seemed to be enough to earn a shock replay, but Blyth weren't satisfied with that. In the best tradition of the cup, a last-minute free kick caused a loose ball which was slotted in by Terry Johnson. Blyth had done it – and they were now on the cusp of a glorious local derby against their neighbours Newcastle.

Except of course, not for the first time, Newcastle blew it. Their chance to face non-league opposition in the fifth round disappeared in a 4-1 fourth round defeat to Wrexham. So it was to North Wales that Blyth headed for what would turn out to be one of the strangest games of all time.

A tremendous performance had given Blyth a 2-1

lead with only one minute of the match remaining. The minnows were only seconds away from a home tie with the mighty Arsenal in the FA Cup quarter-finals. And they were only three games away from winning the trophy – but then Wrexham were awarded a corner.

Having successfully booted the ball out of the penalty area, the Blyth players were incensed when the referee ordered the corner to be re-taken thanks to the fact that the corner flag had collapsed. Once more the kick was taken. Once more the ball was cleared by the Blyth defence. Once more the corner flag fell over.

The third time Wrexham swung the ball into the box, Dixie McNeil forced the ball over the line to score a crushing equaliser. It was the cruellest of blows. Blyth were down – but they still weren't out.

DID YOU KNOW?
Oxford University won the FA Cup in 1874.

It turned out that Newcastle did have a role to play in all this after all. With Croft Park far too small to accommodate the nationwide interest that was now swirling around Blyth's non-league heroes, the venue for the replay was switched to St. James' Park. It turned out to be the right choice, as a scarcely-believable crowd of over 42,000 supporters showed up to see Wrexham take a deserved early two-goal lead.

Terry Johnson pulled one back in the second half, but the equaliser just wouldn't come for Blyth. Wrexham had squeaked through by the narrowest of margins to meet Arsenal in the quarter-finals. Some consolation for the Blyth supporters may have come in the fact that the north London giants defeated Wrexham 3-2 and went on to reach the final, where they lost 1-0 to Ipswich Town.

As for Blyth, the players received £350 worth of furniture from a local showroom and a couple of players in that glorious team signed for Newcastle, though there was little long-term progress.

Blyth now play two rungs below the football league while Terry Johnson, scorer of so many of the goals that propelled the club to the most extreme FA Cup run of any non-league side, still turns out for Blyth. Not on the football pitch, though, but in the local market where he runs the fruit and veg stall.

EXTREME GOALS

How Manchester City got into double figures – without the help of Arab backers

No team has got the scoring into double figures in the history of the Premier League – though there's been some close-run things. Manchester United came nearest back in 1995 when they banged nine past a hapless Ipswich Town who, deservedly, were relegated at the end of the season. To find out the last time a team scored ten in the upper echelons of the game, you have to go back to 1987.

DID YOU KNOW?

The fastest England goal in history was scored just 17 seconds into a 10-0 friendly win over Portugal in Lisbon on 27 May 1947. Chelsea's Tommy Lawton was the lucky goalscorer.

Who could have achieved such an incredible tally? Perhaps Liverpool in their Dalglish-era pomp? Or maybe a free-flowing vintage performance from Brian Clough's Nottingham Forest? No – for the answer, we have to travel down to the old Second Division and Maine Road, Manchester, the former home of City in an era long before multi-squillionaire Middle Eastern owners and Brazilian strikers.

It was proving to be a pretty ho-hum season for City, managed at that time by Mel Machin. They were mid-table but were still expected to win against Huddersfield, who were already bottom of the table by a mile and who on that day were bedecked in disgusting yellow-and-black checked away shirts.

Huddersfield had the better of the game in the first half, before a long-range strike by Neil McNab opened the floodgates for City with three more goals coming before half-time.

Starting the second half 4-0 down, Huddersfield nevertheless commendably continued to attempt to play attacking football until Adcock and Stewart made it six with over twenty minutes still to play.

The idea of slowing down the pace and cruising at six goals up was the furthest thing from the mind of the City players, however. Within 60 seconds of the restart after Paul Stewart's goal, Tony Adcock claimed his hat-trick. Not to be outdone, Stewart continued to keep up, reaching his own hat-trick with a tap-in to make it eight goals without reply.

Would the match ball have to be shared two ways? It turned out that there would be further competition as David White scored his second in the 82nd minute before a one-on-one with the no doubt suicidal Huddersfield keeper in the last minute meant that three players had grabbed a hat-trick in one game – an unprecedented event. And as for Huddersfield? Well, just before White's final goal they were awarded a penalty, with Andy May scoring possibly the most pointless goal of all time. They were nine goals down at that point.

It should have been the start of a soaring run to promotion for City, but in fact the game turned out to be a one-off. Paul Stewart went on to have a chequered career at Spurs and Liverpool and David White, his career sadly blighted by injury, ended up playing for Sheffield United and Leeds. Tony Adcock was only to stay at the club a few more weeks before he moved to Northampton Town in January in exchange for Trevor Morley.

After that monumental game it seems that perhaps the players were exhausted. City embarked on a disappointing run only two wins in seven games after Christmas, and even somehow contrived to lose 1-0 to Huddersfield in the return fixture in April. It must have been of some consolation for the Yorkshire side to take three points off Machin's men, but after letting in ten, you could hardly call it revenge.

DID YOU KNOW?

The record number of Football League goals scored in a single day is 209, scored on 2 January 1932 in 43 matches.

EXTREME GOALS II

How Stirling Albion scored more goals in one professional British game than anyone else in the 20th century

On the face of it, there wasn't a lot of glamour involved in a Scottish Cup tie between Stirling Albion, at that time languishing in the bottom division of the Scottish league, and Selkirk of the Border Amateur League in December 1984.

Supporters of Albion had little cause to believe the game would be a shoo-in. They'd won only four games all season and were understandably nervous at the prospect of playing an unknown quantity. Little were they to know just how easy it would be.

Selkirk, it should be said, were doomed from the start. The small team from an eastern Scottish town were forced to field their reserves on that fateful day. The first team had, due to financial problems, temporarily folded and so the Selkirk Vics were promoted to take over first-team duties and allow the club to keep its place in the Scottish Cup. They probably wish they hadn't bothered.

A mere 371 spectators turned up on a freezing December afternoon to see Alex Smith's side rack up a comfortable 5-0 advantage by half time. It was something of a surprise to the gaffer. His scouting team had been to watch Selkirk only a few weeks before, and in that match the minnows had raced into an early 3-0 lead. This kind of total capitulation wasn't meant to be on the cards at all.

Whatever happened in the Selkirk dressing room at half time is probably best left to the imagination, as in the second 45 minutes they fell apart in a way that has never been repeated. As Stirling went on the rampage, scoring roughly once every three minutes, textile worker Richard Taylor, Selkirk's hapless keeper, let in another fifteen goals. Yes, you read that right. Fifteen.

As the mud on the Annfield pitch became increasingly

boggy, the Selkirk players seemed to almost disappear in the encroaching gloom. Willie Irvine scored five and winger Dave Thompson scored seven. Eight different players got on the score sheet for Stirling by the time the 90 minutes were up in the most extreme British football score of the 20th century. The final result was that poor old Selkirk lost by a staggering twenty goals to nil.

Pilgrimage to the site of this ultimate extreme result doesn't give much of a sense of what it must have been like on that chilly afternoon. Annfield was sold off to become a housing development in the early 1990s. Stirling still rattle around in the lower reaches of the Scottish league while the Selkirk manager on that fateful day, Jackson Cockburn, took probably the only sensible measure after the worst day of his club's sporting life. He emigrated to Qatar.

Selkirk did eventually recover from their financial plight, however, and now play in the East of Scotland League. But, a quarter of a century on, Cockburn still feels the scars. 'Every year I wish that some team will win 21-0 and take the record away from me,' he said in an interview in 2005. 'You can't take away the fact that it was the worst result of the 20th century. I just wish it had never happened.'

DID YOU KNOW?

When Dundee Harp beat Aberdeen Rovers 35-0 in a Scottish Cup first round tie on 12 September 1885, everyone must have believed they had witnessed a record score that wouldn't be beaten for years. But, incredibly, on the same day and in the same competition Arbroath beat Bon Accord 36-0 – and that is still the biggest winning margin in British football history.

EXTREME OLD AGE

How the vainest of chairmen and the most desperate of managers got themselves into the record books

Not since the days of the Charlton brothers has it been a regular occurrence to see bald players on football pitches. Indeed, in an era where players often look like they would be more suited to a career on the athletics track than the football pitch, there is less and less room for the bald, the ailing and the slow to make their mark, despite the often sublime skills shown by the likes of Chris Waddle and Peter Beardsley in the last few years of their careers.

Stanley Matthews was an incredible 50 years of age when he made his last playing appearance but even he isn't the record holder for the oldest player ever to appear on a British football pitch in a senior level game. For that we need to look firstly to the late Neil McBain, who takes the crown for an appearance in an English league match.

A prestigious playing career as a full-back took in stints at Everton, Liverpool and Manchester United as well as three caps for Scotland during the 1920s. McBain was known for his sublime ball skills and for possessing the ability to head a ball with extreme power – no mean feat in an age when footballs were often more like bowling balls than the light, responsive balls we see today.

Long after his playing days were behind him, and while working as manager of New Brighton FC in 1947, McBain was presented with a goalkeeping crisis. With absolutely nobody else available, it must have been with a fair degree of trepidation that, at the grand old age of 52 years and four months, McBain ended up playing between the sticks himself for a Third Division North game against Hartlepool in March 1947.

Perhaps inevitably, the performance itself was less than perfect. McBain picked the ball out of the net three times as Hartlepool strolled to victory. He then went on to manage Watford, Leyton Orient and even had a stint in Argentina as manager of Estudiantes de la Plata. He died in 1974.

DID YOU KNOW?

Goalkeeper John Burridge is the oldest player ever to have played in the Premier League, appearing for Manchester City in 1995 at the age of 43 years, four months and 26 days.

McBain may have played out of necessity, but the record holder for a senior level game played for reasons more to do with vanity than emergency.

While Doncaster Rovers endured a spell out of the league in 2003, a certain John Ryan was selected as a substitute for the Belle Vue side's away match against Hereford United at Edgar Street on 26 April. He never played for Rovers again after that match and he was only on the pitch for three minutes. His identity would probably have been a mystery to many neutrals in the crowd. So the question is, why would manager Dave Penney select a man who was aged 52 years and eleven months to take part in a Nationwide Conference match? Easy. He was Doncaster Rovers' chairman.

Making his fortune out of a chain of cosmetic surgery clinics, Ryan, a lifelong fan of the club who had always dreamed of playing for 'Donny', came on during injury time of his club's 4–2 win. He told reporters afterwards: 'I came on when the ref put his board up for an extra three minutes of injury time. I didn't actually get a kick of the ball but I had a good run around.'

It must have been hard for Penney to refuse Ryan's request. After all, if the boss wants to come and work on the shop floor for a while, it's probably not in the best long-term career prospects of the gaffer to refuse. Penney stayed on at Doncaster, now back in the Football League, until 2006. Ryan is still chairman, though – perhaps wisely – has so far confined his 'skills' to the boardroom since that day.

EXTREME CUP REPLAY

How Oxford City and Alvechurch took over ten hours to resolve a cup tie

The concept of the endless cup replay is an entirely alien first-hand experience to anybody under the age of 30 nowadays. Before the early 1990s, when this eccentricity was abolished by the FA, it was one of the great oddities of the FA Cup. Penalty shoot-outs, golden goals; these were all considered to be dangerous modern trends. If two teams playing each other in a cup tie should happen to draw after extra time then there would be a replay. And if that game also ended in stalemate, then there would be another replay. And another, and another...

The last of these endless cup replays occurred back in 1991 when it took Arsenal and Leeds four games to settle a tie. But for the all-time record, we have to head back to 1971 and a first round tie between Oxford City of the Isthmian League and Alvechurch of the Midland Combination League.

Nobody in the crowd that rolled up on Saturday 6 November to Lye Meadow, the home of Alvechurch (complete with that staple FA Cup eccentricity of a sloping pitch that invariably gets referred to as 'notorious'), could have known that it would be another 588 minutes before they'd see the winning goal.

Two down at half time, Oxford City revived in the second half with two goals of their own to set up the first replay at the White House ground in Oxford the following Tuesday. Two goals in the first half, one apiece, and a goalless second half meant that a second replay was required, this time at the neutral venue of St. Andrews, home of Birmingham City. 3,600 by now no doubt bemused supporters turned up to see two first-half goals, followed by none in the second half, once again result in a one-all draw.

Four days later on a Wednesday night they tried again, this time at Oxford United's home, the Manor

Ground. By this time the strain was starting to show for the part-time players. Car plant worker Eric Davis could no longer turn out for Alvechurch thanks to his night shift commitments and Oxford City's Eric Metcalfe was forced to take time off from his day job as a schoolteacher after damaging his fibula.

The fourth tie ended goalless. The fifth, once again played at the Manor Ground, was to prove equally frustrating. Incredibly, the full 90 minutes plus extra time ticked by and the score still remained goalless. The teams were required to meet for an unprecedented sixth time, though by this stage the fixture backlog was becoming a major concern. The two teams knew that an away tie with Aldershot awaited the winners. They'd known this since the time of the first replay. So, barely 48 hours after their latest stalemate, the two sides met again on a Monday night.

City's boss, John Fisher, was forced to make changes when the army, who seemed to have grown tired of having to sign endless release forms, refused to let two of their soldiers – who had been turning out for Oxford – play. They were the lucky ones. One elderly Alvechurch supporter collapsed and died during the last game at the Manor Ground. He was never to know that he was only one game away from finally seeing a conclusion to the most extreme series of cup replays Britain has ever seen.

> **DID YOU KNOW?**
> Cardiff City are the only non-English team to have won the FA Cup, lifting the trophy in 1927.

Bobby Hope was the man who finally ended it all, netting in the 16th minute of the fifth replay for Alvechurch. It would turn out to be the only goal of the game. It had taken six attempts, but finally there was a winner. For some Alvechurch players, the marathon, coupled with their league games, meant they had played 12 games in three weeks.

Sadly, though, Alvechurch failed to capitalise, losing 4–2 in the next round to Aldershot. There were suggestions afterwards that T-shirts should be printed for the supporters who had attended all six games – the original tie plus all five replays. Though as Graham Almer, who appeared in an Alvechurch shirt in all six of the matches, explained, the bond between the two clubs went way beyond a novelty slogan printed on cotton.

'We didn't know the Oxford players at the start, but we were on first-name terms at the end,' he recalled. 'We were turning up as if long-lost mates – the same teams, the same players, the same result. It was character-hardening. Tactics went out of the window. We just carried on playing the same way.'

EXTREME ABSENTEEISM

How Scotland thought they'd won the easiest international match of all time

There has been precious little for Scotland supporters to cheer about in recent years. At the time of writing it's been over a decade since they qualified for an international tournament and, even on the occasions when they have made it to the World Cup or European Championships, they've proved adept at either sustaining the worst of luck (getting knocked out of the 1974 World Cup in West Germany without losing a game) or suffering the most ignominious of defeats (Costa Rica in

Italy in 1990 and Peru in the 1978 World Cup in Argentina being perhaps the two most embarrassing examples). But there was one game on the road to the 1998 World Cup in France that even Scotland thought they couldn't lose…

An away game in Estonia looked on paper like a potentially tricky tie for Craig Brown's men. It was October 1996 and confidence in the Scotland camp was fairly high. Having just beaten Latvia 2-0 they were off on a short journey down the Baltic to Tallinn where, unbeknown to the squad, the most almighty of off-pitch rows was about to ignite.

When Scottish officials arrived at the stadium they were nonplussed to find that the floodlights were nothing more than temporary structures mounted on lorries. This, coupled with a 6:45pm kick-off, gave rise to major concerns that the goalkeepers would not be able to see the ball properly as evening descended. Having voiced their objection to the governing body, FIFA, the next morning the decision was made to bring the kick-off time forward to 3pm. Scotland were happy, the fans in the city were informed, but the Estonian officials refused to play ball.

Claiming that they were concerned about security, and pointing out the fact that their players were based 80 kilometres away, they decided that making it to the ground on time would be impossible. The fact that the TV contract they'd signed stipulated a 6:45pm kick-off made the matter academic to them. The match would start at 6:45 and that was that.

With the Scotland players on the pitch, the fans in their seats and the referee about to blow for kick-off, there was still no sign of the Estonian squad. Unperturbed, on the stroke of 3pm the match began. Billy Dodds passed the ball to John Collins. That was all the action the ref wanted to see. He blew the final whistle, to cheers from Scotland fans and players alike. FIFA rules dictated that should the opposition not turn up, they would be automatically punished with a 3-0 loss. Scotland had thrashed them. And the game had lasted no more than about two seconds.

This being Scotland, however, things were never going to be as easy as that. A subsequent FIFA meeting decided that the match should be replayed after all, in the neutral venue of Monaco. It finished goalless. Scotland still qualified for the World Cup in France (before going out in the first round, of course) but never has the phrase 'there was only one team in that game' been more appropriate.

DID YOU KNOW?

The first international match not involving a British side took place in New Jersey, USA, on 28 November 1885. The USA played Canada, with the Canadians winning 1–0.

EXTREME GOALSCORING

Why scoring a hat-trick really isn't anything much to shout about if you're a Luton Town fan

One of football's most-repeated maxims is that young players need time to settle into the first team. They need a good few games to adapt to the faster pace, to lose their rawness and to mature slowly into a vital component of the first XI. Well, clearly nobody told the striker fielded by Luton Town on Easter Monday at their home Kenilworth Road in 1936.

DID YOU KNOW?

The record for the most Football League career goals belongs to Arthur Rowley. From 1946 to 1965 he scored 434 League goals in 619 matches for West Bromwich Albion, Fulham, Leicester City and Shrewsbury Town.

A fringe player in the Luton set up, Joe Payne, a wing half and former coal miner, had spent much of the previous few seasons loaned out at Biggleswade Town. He then came to manager Ned Liddell's attention as a player who could fill in during an injury crisis so, to the surprise of many supporters, he was named in the starting line up to play as centre forward for a match against Bristol Rovers. He'd only made three previous appearances in the first team and wasn't even named in the match programme that day, coming in only as a late replacement for the injured Billy Boyd.

The 22-year-old delighted Liddell and supporters alike by netting the first goal. Roberts then made it two. Surely nobody could ask for more from Payne? He'd scored on his debut and it was only natural that he would begin to tire in the second half. But then all hell broke loose.

Starting just before half-time and ending five minutes before the end of the match, Joe scored TEN goals in 63 minutes. Seven of the goals were scored with his feet and three with his head in a performance that has never been repeated to this day. A team-mate with the surname of Martin, who clearly must have thought this was all just a bit silly, scored in the last minute to even out the bragging rights a tad. But there was no doubt that it was Payne's day as the match ended with a final scoreline of 12-0.

Unsurprisingly, interest from other clubs in the man who had made this most jaw-dropping of debuts came thick and fast and it wasn't long before Payne was capped by England (he scored twice against Finland) whilst keeping up his penchant for goalscoring at Luton, netting an awesome 55 goals in 39 games to earn promotion for Luton the following season.

A big-money move to Chelsea followed. The timing, however, was appalling. The Second World War broke out, Payne broke his ankle twice, and despite a brief spell at West Ham after the war, his career faded. Payne died in 1974 but he's never been forgotten at Kenilworth Road, with one of the executive suites named in honour of him to this day.

Joe Payne may have been destined to never be able to live up to that incredible goalscoring performance, but let's put this into context. 'Striker' Brett Angell scored one goal in 19 appearances for Everton a few years back and Jason Lee scored fifteen in 94 appearances for Nottingham Forest. That's only five more than Payne managed in an hour. Shame on you both.

EXTREME CULTURE SHOCK

How the world's most secretive regime ended up in Middlesbrough

In these days of international TV, sporting rights syndication, inter-continental transfers and global branding in football the concept of the beautiful game as a culture shock is becoming increasingly implausible. Just as players from Togo and Paraguay ply their trade in the Premier League, so international tours by British teams to the likes of Malaysia and Japan are an increasingly mundane pre-season routine in the footballing calendar.

Gone are the days when teams located anywhere east

of Vienna were described by commentators as an 'unknown quantity' during international tournaments. But some things, however, don't change. North Korea, as the world's most isolated regime, is one of the few places left on earth where it can be assumed that the population's knowledge of the outside world is close to non-existent – and that includes the footballers.

Indeed, the exposure to the outside world that the 2010 team had received ahead of the South African World Cup was scarcely more advanced than that of their 1966 equivalents. Yet while the current crop played games in the cosmopolitan hubs of Johannesburg and Cape Town, the squad that travelled to England in 1966 headed to Middlesbrough – a town where the locals and their visitors experienced a mutual culture shock that simply couldn't be repeated now.

DID YOU KNOW?

The first non-white England player was a chap called Frank Wong Soo, who had a Chinese father and an English mother. He made his international debut on 3 February 1945, a full 33 years before Viv Anderson became the first black footballer to play for England.

Since the Korean War of 1953 the People's Republic of Korea had completely isolated itself from the outside world. To the point where other nations in their World Cup qualifying group refused to even recognise them as a country – a situation that led to both legs of their 9-2 aggregate thrashing of Australia taking place in Cambodia.

Arriving in the UK, the team headed up to Middlesbrough on a train. Archive footage shows swarms of confused locals in flat caps and winkle-pickers asking the shell-shocked players for autographs. 'The people of Middlesbrough supported us all the way through,' recalled Rim Jung Song. 'I still don't know why.'

With an average height among squad members of five foot five and with training taking place in the humble surroundings of Billingham Synthonia FC, the first game at Ayresome Park, home of Middlesbrough FC, against the Soviet Union, ended predictably – with the vastly more physical Russians demolishing the Koreans 3-0 in front of an unprecedented crowd of 22,000.

The second game was a vast improvement. Perhaps taking inspiration from the Dear Leader Kim Il Sung, who had advised the players before their departure for England to '…run swiftly and pass the ball accurately', they held Chile to a creditable one-all draw.

The final game looked to be North Korea's swansong – a tie against a fearsome Italian side. The game itself was the moment that the people of Middlesbrough, who had turned out in incredible numbers to support the most ultimate of all underdogs, got the match they wanted. Against all the odds, Pak Do Ik scored the only goal of the game to send his country through to the second round.

Nobody in the crowd at Ayresome Park that day could quite believe it. 'They played good football,' recalled one fan. 'They were like a team of jockeys.'

So a team that almost had almost been refused visas to enter the UK by the Foreign Office travelled to Goodison Park in Liverpool for a second round tie against Portugal, a team which included the mighty Eusebio. Thousands of Teessiders travelled down for the match, which saw the North Koreans soar into an incredible 3-0 lead before Portugal's greatest ever player led a second-half comeback to win 5-3.

Never again will England see an international team with such little exposure to the world beyond their own borders. While Ayresome Park, venue for that incredible win over Italy, may now be a housing estate, there is one small reminder of that incredible goal by Pak Do Ik. The front garden of one of the new houses contains an actual-sized bronze boot. It's a sculpture by the artist Neville Gabie, and it marks the exact spot where the ball was struck to hit the winning goal — a goal that made an industrial northern English town fall in love with a team that may as well have come from another universe.

EXTREME DOWNFALL

How a Scottish village side went from part-time nobodies to Europe and back again within six years

'Be careful what you wish for' is an adage that seldom applies to football. Cup wins, promotion, 30-goals-a-season strikers... perhaps too many fans these days are happy to remain myopic about the long-term wellbeing of their team as long as the good times begin as soon as possible.

The monumental debt of the biggest clubs in Britain right now is a cause for concern to many of the football fans whose loyalty goes beyond their next Sky Sports subscription. And while it's true that the day will probably never come when the likes of Chelsea or Manchester United wind up in the receivers' court, the story of Scottish borders club Gretna FC is perhaps the ultimate modern footballing tale of what can happen when a club's fans get everything they ever asked for overnight – but with no Plan B.

Situated right on the English/Scottish border, Gretna's geographical extremity meant that they spent the majority of their existence in the depths of the English non-league pyramid. Seemingly rooted forever at the sort of level that you would expect a club situated in a town with a population of less than 3,000 to be, they could not have guessed that their whole world would end up being blown apart through the ownership of millionaire Brooks Mileson.

Making his millions in construction and insurance, it was under Mileson that the club were elected to replace Airdrieonians in the Scottish League in 2002 – their third attempt to enter a league which still maintains a 'closed shop' policy to teams outside of the pyramid except in the instance of another club going bankrupt.

Put quite simply, Gretna took Scottish football by storm. With Mileson's wallet attracting the best players from outside the top flight, two successive promotions saw Gretna find themselves just one rung under the

Scottish Premier League in 2006. Their tiny Raydale ground was heaving at every game and the fans knew that an appearance in the Scottish Cup final against Edinburgh giants Hearts could provide the means for the tiny border village to enter European football. They were in dreamland.

Tens of thousands of Gretna fans were at Hampden for the club's greatest ever day and, despite losing the final in a penalty shootout, they sneaked into the UEFA Cup through the back door. Hearts had finished second in the Scottish Premier League that season and so had already done enough to enter the UEFA Champions League. As they obviously couldn't enter both European competitions it was left to Gretna, as losing Scottish Cup finalists, to enter the UEFA Cup, where they drew Irish side Derry City as opponents for their first round qualifier.

Gretna may have swept away pretty much everything in their path over the previous four years but unfortunately in European football they finally met their match, with Derry racing to a 7-3 aggregate victory over two legs.

Promotion to the Premier League back in Scotland came the next year, but with the Raydale ground falling well short of the standards required for top-flight clubs, Gretna were forced to play all their home games at Fir

Park, Motherwell — a ground situated over 75 miles from Gretna itself.

It was a dismal season. The gulf in quality between the SPL and the lower Scottish leagues was pronounced and after a 4-0 opening day defeat to Falkirk, poor Gretna remained rooted to the bottom of the division for the rest of the season.

Then the worst bombshell of all fell on this already most fragile of clubs. Brooks Mileson became seriously ill and his family immediately severed all ties with the club — including their financial support. The effect was instantaneous. The club imploded.

Wages stopped being paid and it took the SPL stepping in to guarantee the players their money and enable Gretna to limp to the end of the season. Crowds, already absurdly low for a club in the top division, dropped to an all-time Scottish Premier League record low of just 431 for a 'home' game against Inverness Caledonian Thistle in April 2008.

Administration and liquidation swiftly followed at the end of the season, with Gretna being replaced in the Scottish league by Annan Athletic.

Supporters rallied immediately, forming a brand new club called Gretna FC 2008 Ltd. Playing at the Everholm Athletics Complex in, ironically, nearby Annan, the new team began the 2008/09 season with a cup game against

Craigroyston. Since then Gretna have returned to their Raydale home, whilst Brooks Mileson never recovered from his illness and died in November 2008.

From UEFA Cup football to the East of Scotland League in two years is a downfall that was unprecedented in British football. Gretna fans, perhaps more than any other football supporters, are painfully aware of just what can happen when your club's only source of income comes from just one individual. Chelsea fans – take note.

EXTREMELY STRANGE STANDS

Why Southampton made it possible to watch football from inside a chocolate box

Don't be fooled by people who tell you all football grounds these days are soulless corporate entities. For every identikit new stadium (particular offenders being the Britannia Stadium in Stoke and the Deva Stadium in Chester), there are myriad developments that do attempt to inject a bit of originality and innovation into their design.

The atmosphere at Arsenal's Emirates stadium may not have the intensity of the North Bank at Highbury in the 1970s but, on the other hand, football clubs are now attempting to treat fans as customers, not as fools who will tolerate leaking roofs, crumbling terraces and dangerous crushes in order to watch their team.

DID YOU KNOW?

Hampden Park in Glasgow, which opened in 1903, was the largest stadium in the world until the famous Maracanã in Rio de Janeiro was completed in 1950.

Though, despite the attempts of modern architects, it has to be said that genuine eccentricities in terms of football ground oddities are, for better or worse, seriously on the wane. Those that remain should be cherished. Honourable mentions should go to Brechin City, where one side of the ground is still dominated by a huge hedge, with a tiny step of terracing in front of it for spectators. Also to St James Park in Exeter, where the away end terrace is so tiny that all the houses behind it get a fantastic view of the pitch from their living room windows.

Nothing that exists in Britain today, however, can hold a flame to the late 'chocolate boxes' that could be found high above the goal at one end of Southampton's old ground, The Dell.

There had never been anything like it at a British football ground, and there has never been anything like it since. The 'chocolate boxes' took the form of three elevated boxes above the main terracing behind the goal at the Milton Road End of the cramped ground. Each was only able to accommodate around 300 spectators, who would usually be equipped with umbrellas. As was the norm for stadiums up until the 1980s, there wasn't a roof to be seen.

If you managed to arrive early and get to the front of one of the chocolate boxes then the view was absolutely brilliant. If you were late, however, and ended up further back, you'd find that the goal mouth right in front of you would be almost completely obscured by the crowd.

The middle of these three boxes was intended for 'youths', whilst the two to either side were open to all. And there wasn't really a huge amount of logic in the construction of these oddities. For the sake of barely 1,000 extra spectators, the capacity of the terrace underneath the boxes was curtailed thanks to the thick concrete pillars underneath that were needed to keep them upright.

The boxes lasted until 1981 when safety concerns,

based mainly around the steep steps leading to the boxes, led to them being demolished to make room for one single, much larger chocolate box. This in turn lasted until the early 1990s, when for the last few years of the Dell's existence, the entire end was replaced by one all-seater stand.

No doubt supporters are much more comfortable at the shiny new St Mary's stadium, but who could begrudge fans with longer memories occasionally getting wistful for the days when British football grounds were seemingly built by Heath Robinson instead of by slick architectural conglomerates?

EXTREME
GREAT ESCAPE

How an on-loan goalkeeper from Swindon kept England's most northerly team in the league

I've attempted to concentrate on football's lesser-known cases of extremity in this book. There are, however, a few extreme stories that, despite taking place far away from the Premiership, have managed to make their way into national footballing folklore. The fairytale of Jimmy Glass, and its less than perfect aftermath, is a tale that's always worth hearing again. For, quite simply, this was one of the most magical moments football in the UK has ever given us.

Carlisle United had been having an absolute dog of a season. Relegation out of the league looked like a very real possibility when Plymouth Argyle came to town on the last day of the 1998/99 season. Drawing one apiece as the game went into the 94th minute wasn't going to be enough to save the club. Scarborough, whom Carlisle were locked in a battle with to avoid finishing bottom of the entire football league – an ignominy punishable by demotion to the Nationwide Conference – had just finished their home match at the McCain stadium. They'd earned a one-all draw with Peterborough United, enough to keep them up and send the Cumbrian side out of the league for the first time in their history. Or so everyone thought.

At a packed Brunton Park, Carlisle manager Nigel Pearson felt he had no option but to wave every single one of his players up the pitch as the game went into the last 60 seconds of the four minutes of injury time. That included Jimmy Glass, who was keeping goal for Carlisle and playing only his third game for the club as a loan signing from Swindon Town.

Sprinting 100 yards up the pitch, Glass was just in time to make it into the penalty area when Graham Anthony took a corner – almost certainly the very last chance Carlisle would have before the referee blew the final whistle.

As the ball swung into the box, Scott Dobie attempted to head it at the near post. The Plymouth keeper managed to push the ball away, but it only went as far as a totally unmarked Jimmy Glass. With his right foot, Glass made sure the ball sped across the ground and into the back of the net. It's rare enough for a goalkeeper to score a goal. Rarer still that it should be the winning goal in a match. Enter into the equation that this was the goal that saved Carlisle United's football league status and you're in the realms of the most extreme great escape in football history.

In his autobiography, *One Hit Wonder*, Glass described the ensuring chaos. 'Fans were hurling themselves onto the mountain of bodies. Brights [a Carlisle team-mate] grabbed my head. We couldn't breathe. We were screaming: "Get off. GET OFF!"'

As soon as the referee restarted the game, he blew the final whistle. It was 4:55pm on Saturday 8 May 1999 and Jimmy had scored the most dramatic goal in modern British footballing history. At Scarborough, where the champagne was already flowing, the news that they were relegated after all must have been sickening on a level that isn't worth contemplating. Even more tragically, Scarborough never made it back into the league and the club folded in 2007.

But despite their incredible escape that season, it

would be a while before the good times would once again come to Brunton Park. Carlisle eventually did get relegated from the football league in 2004, Jimmy Glass's goal having done little to halt years of consistent underachieving at the very bottom of the league pyramid. United gained promotion back into the league at the first attempt, however, and at the time of writing are enjoying their best spell since the early '80s, riding high in League One.

As for Jimmy, even after his heroics he was never offered a contract by Carlisle chairman Michael Knighton, and he drifted out of the game after a couple of unsuccessful spells at Oxford United and Brentford. He retired from football altogether at the age of 27 and after a spell as an IT salesman now runs a taxi firm in the Dorset town of Wimborne Minster. Talking about his extreme goal, Glass expressed a heartfelt mixture of melancholy and optimism.

'I can't follow it. There'll never be another moment like it. But that goal taught me that you never know what's around the corner. Anything can happen, absolutely anything.'

EXTREME CUP SHOCK SCOTLAND

Why Celtic fans will always have a soft spot for a club that isn't even based in Scotland

Funny place, Berwick. Situated in deepest Northumberland, the town has long been slung to and fro between English and Scottish possession, sometimes with ludicrous consequences. It was, for example, discovered in 1990 that the town was officially still at war with Russia. It turned out that they'd been included separately from England and Scotland in the declaration of war as nobody was quite certain as to which country the town actually belonged to. As they were therefore left out of the peace declaration, too, technically the small town by the river Tweed was at the forefront of the Cold War.

The town's football club, Berwick Rangers, have led a mostly sleepy existence, their only claim to fame being that they are the only club in England to compete in the Scottish leagues. Their ground, Shielfield Park, rarely sees crowds of more than a few hundred, but in 1967, the year of Sergeant Pepper and the Summer of Love, they were victorious in a footballing shock that has yet to be matched in Scottish football. Inverness Caledonian Thistle may have beaten one of the worst Celtic sides of all time 3-1 back in 2000 and Ross County may have beaten the Parkhead side in 2010, but this result from over 40 years ago is still the benchmark.

In 1967 Glasgow Rangers were, as they are now, one of the giants of the Scottish game with a formidable starting eleven that included deadly finishers in the form of George McLean and Jim Forrest.

Berwick manager Jock Wallace was the mastermind behind this most extreme of cup shocks. A noted disciplinarian, his training methods including making the lads run through sand dunes on the Berwickshire coastline.

The impeccable fitness of his players paid off. In front of 13,365 (a record for Shielfield Park that still stands to this day) Sammy Reid split open the Glasgow Rangers defence to put Berwick in front after barely half an hour.

The second half performance saw Berwick bravely attempt to keep on attacking, rather than taking the safer option of putting everybody back in defence. As the clock ticked down, the supporters of lowly Berwick began to believe the impossible was in fact possible.

In those days, injury time was entirely at the referee's discretion. This made for the embarrassing scenario of Glasgow Rangers captain John Reid begging the ref to allow play to continue for another minute. The ref responded, 'I've given you four already.'

And so, the final whistle eventually did blow on a quite exceptional cup shock. For Glasgow Rangers strikers McLean and Forrest the humiliation called time on their careers at the club. Virtual ever-presents in the first eleven, after this game they never played for the club again.

DID YOU KNOW?

When Rangers lost 3-2 to Hibs in the Scottish Cup quarter-final in 1896, keeper John Bell took it very personally. Blaming himself for the defeat, he changed without speaking to anyone and walked away from the ground, never to return.

Berwick went to Easter Road, Edinburgh, to play Hibernian in the next round, narrowly losing by only one goal. Glasgow Rangers made up for some of their blushes by making it to the final of the European Cup Winners Cup later that season, where they played Bayern Munich.

Jock Wallace, by the neatest of footballing ironies, went on to manage Glasgow Rangers in the 1970s, leading them to numerous league titles and cup triumphs. His greatest triumph, though, will always be the day that a team of sand-dune-wading part-timers pulled off the most extreme cup shock Scotland has ever seen.

EXTREMELY BAD SEASON

How Derby County became a record-breaking type of terrible – but yet still managed to take four points from Newcastle

What constitutes a terrible season? Administration? A mystery fire at the ground? Links with signing Titus Bramble? Derby County didn't have serious money worries, arson or transfer rumours linking them to dodgy centre backs in 2006/07. Though they perhaps wished they could have had some of those excuses come the end of the season, when they became the worst team in modern English footballing history –

racking up a grand total of one win. Yes, that's one win in 38 games of football. That's bad enough to make even fans of the San Marino national side feel a bit better.

Promotion to the Premier League from the Championship is a bigger leap than ever these days, and since the early 1990s there have been quite a few promoted clubs who have crashed and burned spectacularly. Mentions must go to Swindon Town in 1993/94, who let in over 100 goals in their one and only season in the Premiership, and Sunderland, who accrued a measly 15 points in a wretched season in 2005/06, with their only win at the Stadium of Light coming just a little too late, on the final weekend of the season.

For Derby County fans, promotion to the Premier League had come way ahead of schedule. Respected Scottish manager Billy Davies took over the club in 2006 and declared upon his appointment that he thought he could build a side capable of challenging for promotion in three years.

But his young side drastically overachieved, reaching the Premiership via the play-offs in only 11 months thanks to a victory against West Bromwich Albion at Wembley.

Davies believed that elevation to the top flight had

come too soon, and he was to be proved horribly prescient in his predication. One win in 14 games at the start of the season led to Davies parting company with the club before things could get any worse. There was that single win to hold on to, though, a battling 1-0 home victory over Newcastle United in September. Little were fans to know that, if they'd missed that game, they wouldn't see the Rams win again until the following season.

Paul Jewell, ex-Wigan manager, took over reins that were already frayed to breaking point. Performances got substantially worse, though they did collect a point in a goalless draw against Newcastle again, this time at St James' Park. As Easter time neared, it became clear that Derby were almost certainly going to break Sunderland's record low points total of 15, which they'd 'earned' two years previously. Indeed, there was serious doubt as to whether they'd even make double figures at all.

By the time of the final game of the season against Aston Villa, which of course they lost, Derby had racked up an even more impressive litany of failure. They'd made it into double figures – just – but had accrued the lowest points total since Victorian times (when Loughborough had amassed a total of just eight points from 34 games in the 1899/1900 season). They also had the worst goal difference, they had scored the lowest number of goals, and they had the worst goals-per-game ratio in English footballing history, the quickest relegation and the longest winless sequence in Premiership history.

Under Nigel Clough the Rams have now steadied the boat a little and are in the Championship, still battling today to regain their Premier League place. They've even started giving out player of the season awards again. They didn't bother in 2007. The entire squad was considered to be so bad that the award was given to the fans. You can't say they didn't deserve it.

EXTREME FOULS

The most extreme challenges in the game – more suited to gangsterism than football pitches

One of British football's more dismal moments, in the strange torrid times of the early 1990s, was a dodgy shoestring-budget video released by *enfant terrible* wannabe Vinnie Jones. Entitled *Soccer's Hard Men*, the film was an utterly appalling montage of Vinnie, talking with the kind of knuckle-dragging charisma that has served him so well in the Hollywood career that would follow his retirement from football, about what constitutes a true 'hard man' in the game. He also showed us how he managed to deliberately hurt players on the pitch – a trade secret that brought down the full, albeit ultimately feeble, wrath of the FA upon him.

The truth is, however, that much of Vinnie's bravado was just posturing. He never did anything as destructive as a certain Rochdale centre back whose name is lost in the mists of time. It was he who kicked Everton legend Dixie Dean, at that time playing for Tranmere Rovers, so hard in a game in the 1924/25 season that Dixie lost a testicle. The crunching challenge came after the 17-year-old prodigy was warned, 'If you score again, it'll be the last goal you ever score'. Unfazed, Dixie netted again. The revenge tackle was swift and led to the teenager being rushed to hospital for the most delicate of operations.

DID YOU KNOW?

In 1994, Eric Cantona was sent off twice in the space of four days – against Swindon Town and Arsenal.

A mention in this chapter of extreme shame should also go to Willie Young, who committed a foul so appalling that the rules of the game were changed afterwards.

Playing in the 1980 FA Cup Final for Arsenal against West Ham United, it was Young who cynically hacked down Hammers striker Paul Allen when Allen was clean through on goal. At that time there was no law that stated players could automatically be sent off for a tackle from behind, so Young was only booked despite the fact that the foul had clearly prevented Allen from taking advantage of a great goalscoring opportunity. The rules were then changed accordingly so that any future fouls of a similar nature would be punished with an instant red card.

The award for the worst tackle of all, though, for pure malice and a subsequent lack of remorse, has to go to Roy Keane for his eye-watering lunge at Alf-Inge Haaland which ended the Norwegian's career. Manchester United's ultimate warrior hardly had a clean record before his horror tackle in 2001, of course. Keane had already gained a notorious reputation off the back of numerous heavy-handed challenges including a thigh-high shocker on Neil Pointon of Oldham in 1994 that, miraculously, only resulted in a booking. In 1997, during a match at Elland Road, Leeds, Keane damaged his knee ligaments whilst fouling Haaland. The Irishman was furious, but it wasn't until four years later that he managed to get revenge.

Now playing for Manchester City, it was in the

pressure-cooker atmosphere of a Mancunian derby match at Old Trafford that Roy eventually wreaked his revenge in a shocker of a tackle on Haaland's legs. Keane's account of the challenge in his autobiography a year later chills the blood.

'I'd waited long enough. I f★★★ing hit him hard. The ball was there (I think). Take that you c★★t. Even in the dressing room afterwards I had no remorse. My attitude was, f★★k him. What goes around comes around. He got his just rewards. He f★★★ed me over and my attitude is an eye for an eye.'

Haaland never played a full game for City (or any other team) again and he retired from the game in 2003. The legacy of the tackle seemed to be to reinforce public opinion of Keane as being either an uncompromising fighter or a damaged individual who doesn't know where to draw the line. After retiring from the game in 2006, he was sacked his second managerial job as boss of Ipswich Town in January 2011, following an unsuccessful stint in the Premier League as Sunderland manager.

Haaland, now running a property business, is surprisingly supine about his nemesis. In an interview he explained his biggest fear about the most extreme foul in British football: 'The worst thing about what he did, and what he wrote in the book is the example it set to young kids who follow big name players like him. They see these things, and they think it's OK.'

DID YOU KNOW?

In November 1970, Brentford goalkeeper Chic Brodie suffered a serious injury – not as a result of a foul, but after a collision with a dog that had invaded the playing area. The dog decided to chase the ball when it was passed back to Brodie – leaving the player with a shattered kneecap which ended his career.

EXTREMELY BAD TRANSFERS

What a little way a lot of money can go if you buy players like these…

Perversely, there can be something quite reassuring about supporting a cash-strapped football team. Much as you know the gaffer's ability to pick and choose from the best players on the market is severely limited, it's a small comfort to at least know that you're unlikely to experience the unique blend of frustration and anger that comes when a big-money signing goes disastrously wrong.

So it's clubs in the higher reaches of the game that we

must visit in order to find the hubris, expectation and ultimate failure that comes when the gaffer's cheque book comes out for players that simply never even came close to justifying their price tags.

For some of the worst offenders we have to look back to a few '80s transfers of British players to European teams. It was an era when it was still something of a rarity for British players to ply their trade abroad, and it's a surprise that Europe's giants ever looked towards this island of ours again after Luther Blisset's disastrous move to AC Milan. Dubbed Luther 'Miss-it', he scored only five times in his one season there. Dodgy comments about Milan 'signing the wrong black player by mistake' (the rumour being that they actually meant to buy John Barnes) were sadly widespread, and were unfortunately considered acceptable in those thankfully long-ago days.

Liverpool legend Ian Rush had a stinker in a one-season move to Juventus in 1987, famously declaring that being in Italy was 'like living in another country'. He was back at Anfield a year later and stayed until 1996.

And it's certainly not the case that we've always been blessed with the best of foreign talent on our shores, either. Newcastle United fans still flinch at the thought of Brazilian signing Mirandinha, whose two years in the North East were full of injuries, laziness and a seemingly complete inability to realise that he had ten team-mates whom he could pass the ball to.

Thomas Brolin was a skilful Swedish winger who impressed all of Europe during the 1992 European Championships. Leeds boss George Graham managed to lure him to the UK in 1995 but something had apparently gone horribly wrong in the intervening three years. Hugely overweight, and with an attitude set to redefine the word 'petulant', Brolin only made a handful of starts in between allegations of junk food binges and training ground walk-outs. He turned up again at Crystal Palace in 1998 but was deemed so overweight at that point that he was moved to become assistant manager instead. Palace were relegated that same season and Brolin is now a vacuum cleaner salesman back in Stockholm.

Going much further back, the debacle that surrounded Bryn Jones's transfer is noteworthy. Signed by Arsenal from Wolves in 1938 for the then gargantuan sum of £14,000 – a world record at the time – the Welshman had a formidable scoring record for Wanderers and was bought to fill the gaping hole left by Arsenal legend Alex James. Questions were asked in the House of Commons about the size of the transfer fee but it all started well enough, with Jones scoring on his debut.

However, that proved to be the high point of Jones's Arsenal career. He was clearly no replacement for Alex James and the huge crowds that packed out Highbury to see him seemed to have an adverse effect on his confidence. He scored only one more goal that season before he asked Gunners boss George Allison if he could play in the reserves to help him get rid of his big game stage fright. The outbreak of the Second World War put paid to any glorious return to the first team, however, and although Jones stayed at Arsenal until 1949, he only ever scored three more goals for the club.

But for possibly the most dreadful of transfer signings, we must point the finger at Sir Alex Ferguson. The Manchester United boss has done plenty of good business in his quarter of a century in charge at Old Trafford, but on the few occasions he has got it wrong it's been spectacular. Juan Sebastian Veron often gets touted as Sir Alex's worst signing, but goalkeeper Massimo Taibi beats him by a mile. Signings simply don't get much worse than this.

Bought in the summer of 1999 for £4.5 million, it was instantly obvious that Fergie had made an absolute clanger of a decision. Taibi was at fault for two goals scored by Liverpool on the first day of the season. The next week, at Wimbledon, he let in another howler.

Southampton then scored three at Old Trafford, one

of their haul being a goal by Matt le Tissier that trickled over the line after Taibi bungled a save by diving over the ball. Chelsea then knocked five past him at Stamford Bridge and that was that. Fergie had seen enough of Taibi after barely a month between the sticks and the hapless flapper was farmed out to the reserves until Reggina took him off United's hands for two and a half million quid at the end of the season.

Comfortably United's worst ever keeper and the winner of the most extreme bad football transfer simply for the fact that even in the few games he did play for United, there wasn't a single second of a single game where he looked like he was worth even a hundredth of the price Sir Alex so foolishly laid out.

EXTREMELY SHORT ENGLAND CAREERS

Peter Ward, Jimmy Barrett and Stephen Warnock's England careers – all 22 minutes of it

Numerous players over the years have earned just the one solitary England cap – including some pretty good ones if truth be told. It's hard to explain just why players of the calibre of Charlie George and Tommy Smith only won a single cap each in the 1970s, though it may go a long way towards explaining why England went 12 years, between 1970 and 1982, without qualifying for the World Cup.

DID YOU KNOW?

Wayne Rooney broke a 124-year record on 12 February 2003, when he made his England debut aged just 17 years and 111 days. The player who previously held the record as the youngest man to play for England was James Prinsep, who was 17 years and 253 days old when he made his debut on 5 April 1879. Theo Walcott is the current record-holder – on his England debut in 2006 he was 17 years and 75 days old.

But for three players past and present, a full appearance in an England shirt would be something that they could only aspire to. In Stephen Warnock's case, he still can, as at least he is still playing. All three men, however, are notorious for the dubious distinction of having the shortest England careers of all time.

Jimmy Barrett is in this extreme list only by default, as the West Ham man surely would have played more than eight minutes of an England game against Northern Ireland in 1928 if he hadn't got himself injured. The fact that he was in the starting line-up at all at least puts him ahead of these other two examples of breathtaking brevity.

EXTREMELY SHORT ENGLAND CAREERS

Peter Ward was an 85th-minute substitute for an England side strolling to victory against Australia on a fringe tour of the country, which was intended to allow gaffer Ron Greenwood a chance to try out a few new faces prior to the 1980 European Championships in Italy.

Two goals up and with the game petering out, Ward was thrown on and he managed to make a couple of nifty one-twos with Glenn Hoddle. He'd had a good season. A striker for Brighton and Hove Albion, he'd scored 16 goals that season and, at just 24, he could never have expected that his England career would turn out to be so extremely brief.

Australia got a penalty in the last minute to make the final score 2-1. The goal wasn't Ward's fault, but when the ref blew the whistle that was the last England fans would ever see of the bouffant-haired frontman. He'd played for exactly six minutes and 48 seconds.

The next season, Ward moved to Nottingham Forest. The move ended up being a bit of a shambles and Ward quickly sank from being on the margins of the England set up to not even being in the same postal district.

It's more a case of 'watch this space' for Stephen Warnock. The talented Aston Villa defender has so far only managed eight minutes as a sub against Trinidad and Tobago in June 2008. But with England boss Fabio Capello still including him in his squads, it seems likely that Warnock won't be in this list for long. Warnock and Barrett have excuses for their England careers lasting for less time than the average Pink Floyd album track. For Peter Ward, however, now running an English theme pub called 'Scotland Yard' in Tampa, Florida, it must be difficult to keep his temper when smirking expat punters ask him to talk about his 'England career' for the umpteenth time.

EXTREMELY BAD PREDICTIONS

'And you can quote me on that...' How great footballers often have a dodgy relationship with the crystal ball

Football can be numbingly predictable at times. Just as you know that England will go out of a major tournament in the quarter finals, and that Scotland will somehow contrive to snatch heroic failure from the jaws of victory, perhaps it would be better if football managers, players and pundits kept their predications confined to these dead certs. Otherwise they can end up looking rather silly.

The potential future achievement of young players is a common stumbling ground for managers who are often desperately seeking to justify their players' inflated price tags. Ex-Liverpool boss Gerard Houllier made a fair number of dreadful signings during his tenure at Anfield in the early years of the 21st century, but his skewed opinion of Bruno Cheyrou surely must stand as the all-time worst. Upon signing the young Frenchman, Houllier quipped to reporters: 'He will be a winner. He has great skill and some of the things he does remind me of Zidane.'

Comparing poor Bruno with the best player in the world at that time was always going to be something that the youngster would struggle to live up to. As it turned out, it seemed that in Bruno's fleeting appearances for a wretched Liverpool side he wasn't even willing to try. Three goals in 44 appearances before new gaffer Rafa Benitez offloaded him to Marseille on loan upon taking charge meant that Cheyrou's legacy in the pantheon of great French players was more akin to Zebedee from *The Magic Roundabout* than Zidane.

When managers leave the game to enter the world of punditry, they're even more prone to making horrendous gaffes. An absolute peach occurred during the 1998 World Cup in France when Kevin Keegan (no stranger to putting his foot in it anyway) made a solid prediction to commentator Brian Moore as David Batty stepped up to take a penalty kick in a shoot-out against Argentina. If he missed, then England were out. The exchange went as follows:

> Brian Moore: 'Quickly, Kevin – you know him best, will he score?'
> Kevin Keegan: 'Yes.'

Batty didn't, England were out and Keegan, along with the rest of the British viewing public, was left to ponder just how well he knew Batty at all.

Tommy Docherty, ex-Manchester United manager, was forthright in his opinion of Dwight Yorke in 1995, stating: 'If Dwight Yorke is a First Division footballer then my name is Mao Tse Tung.' Fast forward 15 years and Yorke, at the time of his retirement, had played for Manchester United, Sunderland and Birmingham City in a glittering career that saw him score 64 goals for United and be a part of the 1999/2000 Premiership-winning side. Chinese historical scholars have, however, yet to prove that the leader of the Cultural Revolution was in fact a Scottish football gaffer.

Supporters have played their part, too, in some notoriously extreme bad predictions. Milwall chairman Reg Burr was confident that the hooligan element of the club's fan base would behave themselves prior to a match against Derby County in 1984. 'I think our fans know how to behave. I don't believe there will be any problems. Those days are behind us now.' Cue one riot, started by the very same South London fans that were supposedly well versed on how to conduct themselves.

There's something about European competition that seems to make managers of British clubs unusually cocky. Prime position here must go to Malcolm Allison, who predicted that his Manchester City side would 'terrify the cowards of Europe' upon their first ever venture into the European Cup in 1968. They were knocked out in the first round and are still waiting for another bite of the cherry over four decades on.

Happily, it's not just the Brits that get it wrong. Here's ex-Bayern Munich manager Uli Hoeness predication before England's 5-1 spanking of the Germans in 2001: 'How are England going to win in Germany? It hasn't happened for 100 years. I have no doubts whatsoever that Germany will quite clearly thrash England. They will easily qualify for the World Cup with this match.'

And Scotland boss Andy Roxburgh unleashed a classic prior to his side's first game in the 1990 World Cup in Italy. 'We have nothing to fear from Costa Rica' was his maxim before taking on the Central American minnows. They lost 1-0, of course, and went out in the first round.

EXTREMELY BAD PREDICTIONS

Pride of place, however, goes to Geoff Hurst, a name known even to people who don't have the slightest interest in football solely for his hat-trick for England in the 1966 World Cup final against Germany. Geoff didn't see it that way, though: 'That hat-trick gave me a great start in life, but it is not – it is not – going to be the one thing I'm remembered for.'

Sorry Geoff, but your heroics as a West Ham and Stoke player, great as they were, to say nothing of your stint at the Seattle Sounders, just don't quite cut it in comparison.

EXTREME GOBBLEDYGOOK

When the brain and the mouth have a major falling-out…

Just in the same way that you wouldn't expect Alan Green or John Motson to be any good at taking the ball past four defenders and completing a hat-trick at Wembley, in the same sense it's probably naive to assume that an ex-professional footballer will be able to put forth eloquent and fluent soliloquies on the beautiful game whilst under pressure, live, in a crowded commentary box with just five minutes to go in the Cup Final. But still, there's really no excuse for some of the quite appalling mouth-mangled gaffes that we've had to endure over the years on the TV and radio as some kind of punishment for not actually being at the match in person.

It's almost impossible to award an overall winner in this category – there are simply far too many to choose from – but a list of candidates guilty of some of the most extremely appalling punditry simply must include ITV's Clive Tyldesley, who once remarked on a player during a live commentary: 'He's not George Best. But then again, no one is'. Thanks for clearing that up, Clive.

The recently disgraced Andy Gray has had his moments too. One sublime comment on a tackle was: 'There was no contact there – just a clash of bodies'. There's no sexism in your behaviour either, Andy – just a man asking a woman to put a microphone down his trousers…

Barry Davies, a BBC veteran, once remarked that a player '…must be feeling on cloud seven'. Presumably that would be just before he scored his fourth goal to make a hat-trick, Baz.

And who could forget Motty himself, who, in a shining example of the art of stating the bleedin' obvious once informed us that 'The World Cup is a truly global event'.

Another pundit whose microphone gaffe cost him his career at ITV is, of course, Ron Atkinson. However, his comments weren't always of a racist bent. Asked how he thought one game would pan out, he helpfully told the viewing public: 'I'm going to make a prediction. It could go either way'. This is clearly a man you wouldn't really even want to discuss the colour of orange juice with.

In an uncanny reprisal of one of the most famous lines from *Spinal Tap*, hapless Gary Newbon once informed the public that 'There is such a fine line between defeat and losing'. And there's an even finer one between being unable to grasp the basics of the Queen's English and getting a highly-paid job as a sports pundit, too.

DID YOU KNOW?

During the 1997 Charity Shield match, David Beckham wore a rather unusual shirt. Somehow his name had been misspelled on the back, and so for 90 minutes he appeared as David 'Beckam'. David Bentley fell victim to a similar mistake in November 2007, as he played a whole match against Manchester United with the name 'Betnley' on his back.

Stuart Hall – one pundit known for adding a fair degree of highbrow embellishment to his match reports on BBC Five Live – once asked a retiring player the following question: 'What will you do when you leave football, Jack? Stay in football?' Surprisingly, Hall wasn't asked to help with the interview questions when David Frost met Richard Nixon.

Another Radio Five commentator – whose name is lost to history – also had an attack of misplaced higher learning when he informed the listening masses that 'Emile Zola has scored for Chelsea'. It must have been quite a surprise to the man's relatives. The satirical French author died in 1902.

George Hamilton once welcomed viewers to Spain with the following opening line: 'Welcome to the Nou Camp stadium in Barcelona that is packed to capacity…with some seats left empty'. Apparently when George got back to Blighty he was told his job was completely safe, although at the same time he was, in fact, definitely sacked.

Finally, in terms of sheer 'was he even watching the game at all?' incredulousness, a special mention has to be given to the late, great, Brian Moore. His job was to commentate on the legendary European Cup Final of 1980 when Nottingham Forest, under Brian Clough and Peter Taylor, beat Hamburg 1-0. A dream job for any commentator and one that you'd hope to be able to conclude in a fittingly jubilant style. So how did Brian react when the final whistle went? Well, it's easy: 'And Hamburg have won the European Cup!' He didn't go out in the Black Country much after that.

EXTREME GREEDINESS

**The Chelsea player who simply refused to leave –
even though he wasn't given a squad number**

The case of Winston Bogarde is quite astonishing as the
most extreme story ever of a player putting his wage
packet before his career. Legally, the Dutch central
defender did nothing wrong when he signed a
£40,000-a-week contract with the Stamford Bridge
side in 2000. However, when he fell drastically out of
favour with the club, rather than doing as any other
player would have done and finding a way out, he
simply stayed on until his contract expired – despite

being sent to train with the kids and knowing that his chances of ever being selected for the first team again were about as likely as Cliff Richard being asked to headline the Download festival.

It was Gianluca Vialli who had brought Bogarde to London from Ajax, at a time when vastly inflated wage packets were being thrown around the Premiership far more wantonly than today. Within weeks, however, Claudio Ranieri took over as Chelsea manager and made it clear that Bogarde wouldn't be a part of his first team plans. Winston, however, was adamant about one thing. He was staying put.

'I admit it is a great deal,' Bogarde said in 2004. 'I am committed to Chelsea and I will do my utmost to play in the first team. I will do that until the last day of my contract. And I mean that literally. As far as I'm concerned, Chelsea are committed to paying me the salary that they offered me.'

And what did Chelsea get in those four years, exactly? They got nine appearances, all bar one coming in his first few months at the club. After that, a substitute appearance against Gillingham in a League Cup tie in 2002 was all that Blues fans got to see of their £40,000-a-week man between Boxing Day 2000 and the time his contract finally expired in 2004.

As one of the worst value transfers of all time, this has

to be a strong contender, but it was Bogarde's willingness to ignore everything but his pay cheque that makes this such an extreme story of footballing greed. Even an offer by PSV Eindhoven to spirit Bogarde away from his dire existence was turned down in 2002. Bogarde stated that he would only sign if the Dutch club could match the millions he was earning for hanging around the Chelsea training ground in London.

His frustrations, however self-imposed they may have been, were expressed in an interview towards the end of his time at Chelsea: 'I often have the feeling that I am stuck in some kind of tunnel, that I'm wearing a strait-jacket. All my movements are limited. I can't move, can't turn over, can't even look back. So I walk on, on to the light, to the end of the career, to freedom.'

To the surprise of nobody, Bogarde's contract wasn't renewed and he slipped away quietly to retirement – his reputation in tatters, but with more money than he could ever spend.

DID YOU KNOW?

Everton bought Alan Ball from Blackburn Rovers in June 1966 in the first six-figure transfer deal between English clubs. Andy Carroll currently has the honour of being the most expensive English footballer in the Premier League, following his £35m move to Liverpool in January 2011.

EXTREME
MATCH FIXING

At the end of the day, it's eleven men against eleven men. Unless you're counting the people who have fixed the result beforehand…

Under-achieving managers, egotistical players, training ground punch-ups and avaricious owners plunging clubs into bankruptcy: none of these are exclusive to the modern game. They're symptoms of the corrupt, bilious, parallel reality that is football and they have been around since day one. The same applies to match-fixing. The methods may have become gradually more sophisticated but the allure of filthy lucre has always been a temptation that fans, players and Malaysian betting syndicators have fallen for again and again.

Way back in 1905, Billy Meredith of Manchester City was given a one-year ban from football for trying to bribe a player from another team to lose a game. Well-known for his habit of chewing a toothpick while playing (he claimed it was to aid his concentration while he wasn't smoking!) he exposed almost the entire City squad as being involved in match-rigging activities during his 12 months on the sidelines − a move that led to 17 of his team-mates and manager Tom Maley being suspended. Unsurprisingly, Meredith moved to Manchester United when his ban was up.

In 1963, the *Sunday People* newspaper exposed how the appropriately-named Esmond Million, goalkeeper for Blackburn Rovers, had been paid £300 to let in a hat-trick of goals in a match against Bradford City. The Bradford strikers must have been having a real stinker that day, though, as Million actually only got the opportunity to let in two goals in a 2–2 draw.

The *Sunday People* were at it again the next year, with a scoop headline in April 1964 proclaiming to have uncovered 'The Biggest Sports Scandal of the Century'. Here, it was the turn of David Layne and Peter Swan of Sheffield Wednesday, both of whom were accused of being paid to fix it for the Owls to lose against Everton in a match two years previously. Both players, plus Tony Kay, who had subsequently signed for — yes — Everton in the intervening period, were jailed for four months. Jimmy Gauld, a retired player who was paid £7,000 by the *People* to secretly tape the conversations between him and the three players that led to the scoop, was jailed for four years and fined £5,000 after revealing that he had been involved in many similar scams during his own playing days.

More recently, a bizarre scandal involving betting syndicates and sabotaged floodlights brought home how matches could be fixed despite no players or managers being involved. All it took was a crooked security official called Roger Firth to conspire with an Asian betting ring for Charlton Athletic's game with Liverpool in 1999 to be called off at half-time due to the floodlights failing.

Firth was paid £20,000 to allow saboteurs into the ground, who then tampered with the floodlights. The abandonment of the game meant that, according to the rules of illegal Asian betting syndicates (many of which had direct links to Triad gangs) the half-time result would stand and the gang stood to receive around £60 million in winnings. The game at the Valley marked the third time in a single season that these syndicates had managed to cause Premiership games to be called off at half-time.

Police stated that they found enough circuit-breaking equipment, all bought from DIY stores, in the Asian men's hotel rooms to interfere with another eight matches.

What led to the Metropolitan Police slowly unravelling the scam was the fact that Firth had attempted to bribe another member of the security staff with £5,000 to let the floodlight wreckers into the ground. This led to a police tip-off and the men were all arrested.

Firth and two Malaysians, Eng Hwa Lim and Chee Kew Ong, all pleaded guilty to charges of conspiracy to cause a public nuisance and were handed prison sentences.

But for probably the most serious case of match fixing in British football, we have go back to the first few months of the Great War. Erock 'Knocker' West was handed a highly extreme 30-year ban from the game by the FA for taking part in a match fix whilst playing for Manchester United against Liverpool in 1915. Huge amounts had been placed on United to win by two goals at 7-1 odds.

With United indeed leading by two goals, West was singled out for continually kicking the ball high into the stands – supposedly a ploy to waste time and make sure United finished the game two goals ahead. West protested his innocence in the resulting case, even going as far as to hand out leaflets pleading a miscarriage of justice outside Old Trafford, but he was still handed a ban that wasn't lifted until he was 59 years old. Three other players from each side were also banned with one, United's Sandy Turnball, never playing again. He was killed on the front line during the First World War. A tragic end to the most extreme in a line of match fixing episodes that, contrary to what pundits may say, have a history going back to a time when the game was supposed to be more innocent than it is today.

EXTREMELY USELESS CUP COMPETITION

And you thought the FA Cup had lost its glamour...

There's winning trophies, and then there's winning trophies. Every supporter enjoys a cup win, but they do need to be put into context sometimes. Luckily, British football has done quite a bit over the years to ensure that pretty much every team in existence has had its chance to lift some form of unmemorable silverware. Sadly, however, a lot of these competitions were so lacking in glamour or prestige that there seems to be more than a little embarrassment at some clubs over the dubious cup competitions that they've entered – and sometimes even won. It's the footballing equivalent of having a number one record – in Lithuania.

The Zenith Data Systems Cup is one classic example of total uselessness that dribbled along for a few years in the late 1980s and early 1990s. It was set up as a compensation trophy after British clubs were banned from Europe in the years following the Heysel stadium riot at the 1985 European Cup Final in Belgium.

The competition limped into life with no sponsor, so it was given the title of the Full Members' Cup – named because only teams from the top two divisions (known as full members of the FA) were allowed to enter. There was at least an excuse for the big boys not to enter that season. The clubs that would have qualified for European competition prior to the ban were given a separate cup competition called the Screen Sport Super Cup. Liverpool and Everton contested the two-legged final which ended, to nobody's great interest, in a 7-2 aggregate win for the Reds.

That was that for the not-very-Super cup, and with the top clubs expressing no interest in competing in the Full Members' Cup, the competition was left to the also-rans of the top two flights. Known as the Simod Cup from 1987 to 1989 and then as the glorious Zenith Data Systems Trophy before being abolished in 1992 when clubs were allowed back into

Europe, the games actually threw up some pretty good finals.

Perhaps due to the lack of pressure on the clubs, some of the highlights included a cracking 5-4 win for Chelsea against Manchester City and a ding-dong 4-3 triumph for Nottingham Forest against Everton in 1989. Chelsea liked the competition so much that they won it again, beating Middlesborough in 1990. Barely 25 years ago, the Blues took this competition so seriously that they, along with Forest, are the only sides to have won it twice. Handy ammunition for fans of other Premier League clubs!

The last season for the Zenith Data was 1992, when Forest beat Southampton 4-3 in another great final. With English clubs allowed back into the European cup competitions, the Zenith Data Systems Trophy was swiftly scrapped and has barely been mentioned since.

Going further back, the Watney Cup was a trophy that, although probably about as valuable as a scratched Max Boyce record, has actually developed a minor cult reputation in the 40 years since its short-lived existence. Much of this is down to some cracking surviving photos of the beautiful game at the absolute apex of early 1970s kit and hairstyle sartorial splendour (you can't move for Rolling Stones shaggy cuts and classic sponsor-free shirts). There's also a little bit of history tied up in this briefly-contested competition.

For it was in this pre-season tournament, fought over by the highest-scoring team from each division (barring those in the top flight who had qualified for Europe) that Britain's first ever penalty shoot-out took place. The occasion was the 1970 semi-final between Manchester United and Hull City. George Best was the first man up to take a kick, and he scored from the spot. Denis Law missed one and it was Hull goalkeeper Ian McKechnie who blazed the ball over the bar to send Manchester United through to a final – which they went on to win against Derby County.

Penalty shoot-outs became common in the Watney with the '71 and '72 finals both being decided by shoots-outs (Colchester United and Bristol Rovers were the victors) before Stoke City won by more conventional methods in 1973, beating hapless Hull City again by two goals to nil. The competition was scrapped after that, leaving the Potteries side with undoubtedly their most useless piece of silverware.

Even the glorious FA Cup has had some entirely useless amendments in its time. Back in the early 1970s, the bigwigs at the FA chanced upon the idea of holding a third place play-off game for the losing semi-finalists. This is a concept that has thrown up some great games in the World Cup over the years, but it is perhaps a notion that is rather conceited when the teams involved include the likes of Stoke City rather than Brazil.

Not even played at Wembley, the first 'third place' match was watched by a pitiful crowd of just over 15,000 on the night before Cup Final day itself. Manchester United beat Watford 2-0 at Highbury. At least Watford didn't have far to travel, unlike players and supporters of Everton and Stoke City the next season who had to travel to Crystal Palace on a Friday night for the 1971 third place 'spectacle'. 5,000 punters watched Stoke edge past the Toffees 3-2, though it's highly doubtful anyone in attendance who is still alive remembers a thing about it.

The idea limped on for another few years until it reached its nadir in 1974 – barely 4,000 turned up at Filbert Street to see Burnley beat home side Leicester City 1-0. After that, the whole idea was thankfully put to sleep for good. The local paper, the *Leicester Mercury*, described the farce perfectly the next day: 'It was the game neither side wanted. It's obvious that the public couldn't care two hoots.'

But top prize for the most extremely unmemorable cup competition must go to the late, utterly unlamented Group Cup. Don't worry too much if you've never heard of it. Most supporters of the teams that have actually won the thing haven't either.

The Group Cup was a short-lived pre-season competition that ran for a princely two seasons from 1981 to 1983. With no sponsor, no big-name entrants and not even a Wembley final, it was the ultimate non-event. And it really dragged on, too.

It was set up as a replacement for the Anglo-Scottish Cup, which had whimpered to a halt after Scotland refused to send any more teams, voicing their frustrations about the lack of top English sides willing to compete. So the Group Cup roared into life on August 15th 1981 in front of spectacularly sparse stadiums. A mighty 658 turned up at Burnley and 1,567 at Shrewsbury Town for their first games.

32 teams entered the competition, which was split into eight regional groups. Only one team from each group could go through to the next round which meant that, in this most meaningless of all competitions, there were some games where both teams knew that they wouldn't go through regardless of the scoreline. It really must have been a truly unique atmosphere – enough to make any supporter reach for a Sartre novel or some Prozac. Even the managers seemed to fall into some kind of ennui. Leyton Orient boss Jimmy Bloomfield had this to say after his side got knocked out: 'In this kind of competition

you definitely get some strange results. The crowd don't feel the same about it, and neither do I or the players.'

Strangely, the competition was then halted until December, and the final wasn't played until the next April. Blundell Park, Grimsby, was the venue for the first final, which saw the Mariners beat Wimbledon 3-2 in front of barely 3,000 people.

You'd think that the bigwigs at the FA would have acted quickly to put this horror show out of its misery. But if you *do* think that, you clearly haven't got the first idea about the FA. Of course the Group Cup came back the next year, to equally empty stadiums up and down the country. In 1983 it was Lincoln City who earned themselves the chance to stage the final of the most useless cup of all time, and they duly lost 3-2 to Milwall.

By that time, the FA had cobbled together a new competition just for clubs in the bottom two leagues which, with typical slick panache, they'd named the Associate Members' Trophy. This morphed into what is now the successful Johnstone's Paint Trophy. But what of the Group Cup? Is it still languishing in the trophy cabinet at the New Den? Or is it, more appropriately, now being used as a bookend by a former board member of the Lions who just can't be arsed to take it to the charity shop? Answers on a postcard please.

EXTREMELY
LONG WAIT

Why we're still waiting to find out the winners of a British cup competition after 23 years

The Anglo-Scottish Cup was devised as a pre-season knockout competition for the best teams in England, Scotland and Ireland who hadn't qualified for Europe. Formed out of the ashes of a short-lived tournament sponsored by Texaco in the early 1970s, the competition never ignited the public's enthusiasm and in 1981 the whole thing collapsed when the Scottish clubs withdrew. You could hardly blame the likes of Glasgow Rangers for believing their players had better things to do – the quality of English entrants had gone from the middling (Newcastle United won the trophy twice) to the minnows (the last final was between Notts County and Chesterfield).

But that wasn't the last breath of the doomed contest. It was very briefly revived in 1987 as the Anglo-Scottish Challenge Cup, partly as there was a feeling that English clubs, now banned from European competition, needed something else to strive for, and also, naturally, because a few demented people thought they could make some money out of it.

By a strange coincidence, neither the English nor Scottish Cup winners that year were footballing giants. So, just a few days before Christmas, a dismal crowd of barely 5,000 turned out at Highfield Road, Coventry, to see the English FA Cup winners, Coventry City, take on Scottish Cup winners St Mirren.

Both managers had promised that the evening would be something of a goal-fest. Sadly for the meagre bunch of spectators inside the ground, nothing of the sort happened. David Phillips opening the scoring for Coventry before Kenny McDowell equalised in the second half for the Paisley side.

With the tie evenly balanced at one apiece, you wouldn't exactly say the tension was palpable prior to the second leg in Scotland. And it's a good job too as, for reasons that have never been fully explained, the second leg at Love Street was never played.

The date was set – 22 March 1988 – but as the time grew closer, it's safe to assume that both clubs quietly realised that the travel expenses, the inevitably poor attendance and a lack of a sponsor for the trophy all spelled out the fact that they could save themselves a bit of money by simply not playing the game.

And there the revived Anglo-Scottish Challenge Cup ended, delicately poised, with nobody to this day able to claim victory. No victory parades with open-top buses, no medals, no banner headlines in the local press. Nothing. Does anybody care? Probably not, but it's not as if either club is exactly short of room in the trophy cabinet. Maybe somebody should start a petition to get the second leg played (preferably with the original players from 1987) at last. Though, with some firmness, I must admit that it's not going to be me.

EXTREME ENGLAND THRASHING

The day Hungary tore England apart in their heaviest ever defeat. And it's not as if they hadn't had prior warning...

Imperial arrogance, tactical naivety, dodgy pre-match gnocchi...whatever means you use to explain it (and I'd definitely plump for the first two), everybody with an interest in the English national team must have known that an away game against Hungary in 1954 wasn't going to be easy. Everybody that is, except the Football Association. Secretary (and later President of FIFA) Sir Stanley Rous stated before the game, 'We will win'.

Where his hubris came from is a mystery as it was only a year earlier that England had been shredded 6-3 at Wembley by the 'Magical Magyars' – the game that should have demolished, once and for all, the myth that England were the best in the world at the beautiful game. Hungary had won the football event at the Helsinki Olympics in 1952, they had recently beaten Italy 3-0 and they were fast becoming the European footballing force to be reckoned with.

DID YOU KNOW?

Alan Mullery was the first England player to be sent off, earning himself the dubious honour during a match against Yugoslavia on 5 June 1968.

England captain Billy Wright recalled that the nonchalance of the England players had continued even to the point where they lined up against each on the pitch before the game's start: 'When we walked out at Wembley that afternoon, side by side with the visiting team, I looked down and noticed that the Hungarians had on these strange, lightweight boots, cut away like slippers under the ankle bone. I turned to big Stan Mortensen and said, "We should be alright here, Stan, they haven't got the proper kit.'"

Ferenc Puskas, referred to by another England player the day prior to the game as a 'little fat chap', was Hungary's star player in an incredible team who showed England, for the very first time, what a team who played improvised passing football could do to a team who relied on more old-fashioned coaching methods. Under Walter Winterbottom, these training ground tactics revolved around running a lot and actually asking star players before the game what methods of attack they felt more comfortable with. Winterbottom couldn't even pick the team himself – that job was left to an FA committee.

On that fateful day in November, the Eastern Europeans waltzed past a shell-shocked captain, Billy Wright, and his England team-mates by six goals to three.

It didn't seem like much was learned in the intervening period between that ignominious defeat and the next match between the two sides, which took place in May the following year. England elected to play Peter Harris and Fulham's Bedford Jezzard as their strike force for the game in Budapest. A strange choice, perhaps, as this was Jezzard's debut appearance, and even Harris, a Portsmouth player at the time, had only been capped once before in a dismal 2-0 defeat to the Republic of Ireland five years previously.

The Hungarian crowd cheered when Ivor Broadis scored for England. Though it may well have been out of sarcasm or pity, seeing as England were a staggering six goals to nothing down at the time. They'd been comprehensively destroyed, yet again – with Hungary's greatest ever player, Ferenc Puskas, scoring two himself, Sandor Kocsis (nicknamed the 'Golden Head' for his aerial abilities with the ball) getting on the score sheet with a brace, a free kick by Lantos and more goals from Jozsef Toth and Nándor Hidegkuti.

Hungary went on to reach the final of the 1954 World Cup in Switzerland, where they lost against Germany. It was the end of what at that time was a world-beating run of 31 matches without defeat, stretching all the way back to 1950.

Given the fact that he was the man who had spearheaded the most extreme defeat in the history of the England football team, players were hugely magnanimous in their tributes when Puskas died in 2006. Jack Charlton had this to say about the man who stands alone as the trailblazer for England's heaviest ever loss: 'He revolutionised the game in this country. From there English football started to think more professionally.'

Nobody has ever inflicted a heavier defeat on England

since that day. But it would be many more decades before this nation woke up to the fact that more advanced coaching methods might possibly be the best way to beat the world's top teams. Some would say that we're still waiting...

DID YOU KNOW?

England players first wore their names on the backs of their shirts during the European Championships in Sweden in 1992.

EXTREMELY BAD MISSES

'And Smith must score…' plus many other extremely catastrophic gaffes in front of goal

All strikers have off days, of course. Sometimes the ball just stubbornly refuses to go into the back of the net, whether it be due to heroic goalkeeping, adverse weather conditions or just simply horrid bad luck.

But there have also been occasions when a goalscoring opportunity has been so badly messed up that supporters are given cause to wonder just how on earth gravity conspired to send a ball that should be nicely nestled in the far end of the net to end up in the stands, somewhere near the corner flag or in a grateful goalkeeper's arms. It's the footballing equivalent of falling off a child's bicycle, aged 35, and the British game is stuffed full of bizarre and horribly important misses. Many have been documented on Christmas stocking-filler videos and DVDs, but some of the most disastrous long-term misses happened long before the days of Danny Baker.

Take Bristol City, for example. They made it to the FA Cup final in 1909, against Manchester United, and were a goal down with only ten minutes to go. Inside right Bob Hardy found himself unmarked in front of goal with only keeper Harry Moger to beat. His shot, however, was so feeble that Moger was able to turn the ball around the post to prevent the equaliser. Bristol City have never reached the final since, making Hardy's miss extremely damaging seeing as it marked the start of 101 years without a cup win.

Moving forward around three-quarters of a century, we come to a moment that all fans of Brighton and Hove Albion will want to forget. A rare appearance in the FA Cup final against Manchester United in 1983 saw the already-relegated Seagulls put on a battling display to hold the Red Devils to a 2-2 draw, with former Glasgow Rangers man Gordon Smith scoring the first goal of the game for the South Coast side.

Then, in the last minute of extra time, Smith was put clean through on goal when Michael Robinson barged past two United defenders and passed the ball over to him. BBC commentator Peter Green screamed '…and Smith must score!' But with the ball at his feet and with only Gary Bailey to beat, he hit the tamest of shots and the ball rebounded off the United keeper's legs. It was the last piece of action in the match. It finished two each and Brighton were destroyed 4–0 in the replay.

Smith's career did recover from this most extreme of bad misses, however. He was top scorer for Manchester City the next season and went on to play in Austria before a stint as St Mirren manager. His autobiography was entitled *And Smith Did Score*.

The award for the most visually spectacular miss must surely go to Ronnie Rosenthal. The Israeli Liverpool player of the early 1990s had the ball at his feet with an open goal in a league match against Aston Villa in 1992. Perhaps hoping to impress the travelling support who were seated behind the goal, he lashed the ball as hard as he could, only to see it hit the crossbar. Liverpool still won the match 4–2 – but the sheer comedy of that miss is the only thing anybody remembers.

But it's a penalty taken by striker Len Davies for Cardiff City that wins gold for the most extreme bad miss in British football history. It was the last day of the

1923/24 season, and if Davies had scored in the final match of the season against Birmingham then the Bluebirds would have won the League title. The fact that he missed meant that they missed out on the title on goal difference. It was the closest league finish in league history and Davies' miss meant that the title went to Huddersfield – by 0.024 of a goal.

The great mystery about this is why on earth Davies took the penalty in the first place. He later admitted that he'd never stepped up to the spot before. Nearly a century on and Cardiff have never come anywhere near as close to being crowned the top team in the country, and even though they're making a decent stab of things in the Championship these days, it doesn't look like this run is going to end anytime soon.

EXTREMELY BAD GOALKEEPING

Moments when that pesky football infamously just wouldn't do what it was told

A football truism, albeit a highly undeserved one, is that a goalkeeper's legacy is more often based on a howling error than a great save. For every Gordon Banks (one of the few goalkeepers whose most famous moment was one of greatness – performing the save of the century for England against Pelé and Brazil in the 1970 Mexico World Cup) there are ten other great keepers whose fame is based not around the hundreds of match-saving moments they've been responsible for, but for the odd occasion when the ball, seemingly momentarily transformed into a block of margarine, squirms out of their grasp.

Let's take Gary Sprake, for example. The Leeds United keeper turned out between the sticks for one of the greatest ever sides to grace Elland Road in the late 1960s and early 1970s, under the legendary Don Revie. Sprake, however, was more usually known to other fans as 'Careless Hands'. This cruel nickname came about at Anfield in 1967 when, in an attempt to throw the ball out to team-mate Terry Cooper, he stopped when he saw Liverpool's Ian Callaghan running towards him. The ball somehow slipped away out of his hands and, to the disbelief of everybody in the ground, went on to spin backwards into Sprake's own net. Liverpool fans sang the Des O'Connor hit 'Careless Hands' at half time and throughout the whole of the second half of the game, and consequently poor Sprake found himself with a nickname his usual competence scarcely deserved. Though, having said that, his performance in the 1970 FA Cup final against Chelsea was dreadful too...

DID YOU KNOW?

England goalkeeper David 'Calamity' James once managed to injure himself when he pulled a muscle in his back reaching for a TV remote control. While at Liverpool, he also missed a game thanks to a repetitive strain injury to his thumb – which he blamed on his computer gaming habit!

Joe Corrigan, gentle giant keeper for Manchester City in the early 1970s, still has a cult reputation among older City fans for his heroics on the famously muddy pitches of that era. His only major gaffe, however, is incredible. He turned his back to the field after a clearance, only to see West Ham's Ronnie Boyce belt a screamer from 45 yards straight past him while he was looking in the opposite direction.

Liverpool FC have had their fair share of accident-prone keepers, though it must be said that the great saves outweighed the gaffes throughout the careers of Bruce Grobbelear and even David James. Not so for Sander Westerveld, though. He somehow contrived to let a 30-yard shot from Dean Holdsworth go through his hands and into the back of the net against Bolton in 2001. Manager Gerard Houllier was so incensed that he bought two new keepers in the following few weeks and Westerveld never played for the Reds again.

Dave Beasant should be known for being the first man ever to save a penalty in an FA Cup final, for Wimbledon against Liverpool in their famous 1-0 win in 1988. Sadly, though, Dave is just as well-known in football circles for sustaining an injury after dropping a bottle of salad cream on his foot at home. He'll also go to the grave unable to live down some of the real howlers he let trickle into the net during his stint between the sticks at Chelsea.

The *crème de la crème* of these came in a game against Norwich where, having already been at fault for the Canaries' first goal, the second was a clanger of such extreme proportions that it looked more suited to a school football game where the token asthmatic kid has been forced to go in goal for the last five minutes.

David Phillips unleashed a tame shot from 30 yards out and Beasant, who to this day surely can't explain his actions, appeared to fall over the ball like a pensioner trying to retrieve a lottery ticket in a mild wind. The ball rolled underneath him and into the net, to the widespread mirth of the visiting Norwich fans and to the apoplexy of Blues fans in the Shed end. Beasant went on to play until the age of 43. By the time of his last appearance, in Brighton and Hove Albion colours, he was the oldest registered player in the league.

But the winner of the most extreme bad goalkeeping award must go to Peter Enckelman for a goal conceded in the most inappropriate of circumstances. Howlers in pre-season friendlies or meaningless end-of-season games can be forgiven. But when you're the Villa goalkeeper playing in a local derby against hated rivals Birmingham City, any kind of mistake is going to be scrutinised and endlessly mocked. And this one really was the worst possible kind of gaffe.

It was September 2002 and the Finn had seen little first-team action for Villa since signing for the Midlands club three years previously. Understandable, perhaps, given that his rivals for the number one shirt were Peter Schmeichel and David James. However, upon being made manager, Graham Taylor decided to give Enckelman more first team opportunities, a decision he certainly wasn't the only one to regret after the most extremely farcical goal ever scored in modern football.

Amid the expected tinderbox atmosphere of an evening game against Brum, Villa were thrashed by three goals to nil. But nobody who was at that game will need any reminding of what the defining moment of the match was.

A goal down in the 77th minute, Swedish team-mate

Olof Mellberg had a throw in, and decided to play a defensive shunt back to his keeper. It should have been the easiest of balls to control for the keeper. Except that, somehow, Enckelman never actually touched the ball at all.

Instead, it simply rolled straight past the hapless Finn, whose attempt to stick a foot out to keep the ball at his feet came to nothing. Far, far too late Enckelman tried to run back to try something heroic but by then the ball was in the back of the net and the Birmingham City supporters directly behind him were going ballistic with glee. One fan went too far and went onto the pitch to gesture at Enckelman who, to give him due credit, didn't react to the jeers.

Villa boss Graham Taylor described the team's entire performance that night as 'terrible', while Steve Bruce, the Birmingham manager at the time, helpfully chipped in with: 'That will probably haunt him for the rest of his life. But he's just got to get over it.'

Enckleman did get over it — but not at Aston Villa. He was sold to Blackburn Rovers two years later and, at the time of writing, is playing for Cardiff City in the Championship. The only mitigating factor in the whole sorry affair is that, technically, the goal probably shouldn't have stood at all. The Laws of the Game dictate that a goal, or own goal, doesn't count if it's scored directly from a throw in and if nobody else touches the ball.

Replays show that it looks likely that Enckleman's foot didn't even make the slightest of contacts with the ball, so the goal should really have been disallowed. Though somehow, this only seems to reinforce the fact that cruelty, combined with gross error, really is the most painful experience any goalkeeper is ever going to have to endure.

EXTREME EXPULSION

The sad tales of clubs whose affairs were so extremely rotten that they had to abandon the season halfway through

Considering the financial profligacy that so many football clubs seem to espouse, there have been surprisingly few cases of clubs suddenly folding mid-season. And those clubs who have suffered this most savage of fates have always tended to be outfits in the lower reaches of the league, and their decline has often been thanks to reasons more to do with decades of slow neglect rather than the sudden implosion that comes with a billionaire owner withdrawing his support, or the immediate fallout of a Black Wednesday or a credit crunch.

Gretna are saved from featuring in this list, as the SFA paid the players' wages to ensure they made it to the end of the season before folding in 2007. Chester City, however, weren't as fortunate. In 2010 they became the first professional club in almost 20 years to be wound up midway through the season. It's the most extreme of disasters a club, and its fans, can suffer, and the almost farcical way in which events can spiral out of control can make even a supporter of the fiercest rival team cringe in shame.

A history spent entirely in the lower divisions, coupled with a recent spell in the top non-league division, the Blue Square Premier, Chester City always struggled to capture the support of the town's football fans. A move away from their traditional home of Sealand Road in 1990 to ground-share with Maccelsfield Town 40 miles away didn't help matters and their new ground, the Deva Stadium, which they moved to two years later attracted the mirth of fans of their fierce local rivals just over the Welsh border, Wrexham, for the fact that almost all of the new ground was actually on Welsh soil.

Liverpool boxing promoter Stephen Vaughan bought

the club in 2001 and, although he was to step down as chairman not long after, Vaughan remained the majority shareholder until the final days of the clubs existence. He is regarded by Chester fans as the villain of the piece, though his track record was far from unblemished before he took the border club over.

It was under his tenure that City's fortunes nosedived to lows not even plundered under the ownership of American Terry Smith in the late 1990s and early 21st century. Fans still shudder at stories that emerged of Smith organising games of American football in training and making the players recite the Lord's Prayer before games for which, despite having absolutely no experience in British football, he picked the team himself.

Vaughan, however, brought a different sort of controversy to the club. After initially taking the club back into the league in 2004 it wasn't long before Vaughan's lack of investment saw the club slump out of the league again in 2009 and enter administration. Even before the following season began, Chester were docked a massive 25 points by the FA after Customs and Excise began expressing doubts as to the financial probity of the club.

Starting the season with relegation already a certainty and with fans deserting the club in droves in protest, the threadbare squad went without their wage packets for

October. Vaughan's part in a VAT scam while chairman of Widnes Vikings rugby team meant that in November he became the very first person to fail the FA's 'fit and proper persons' test and so was forced to hand his shares over to his son, Stephen Jnr.

The horrific way in which the club was being run meant that Chester weren't even given the £30,000 sum that all clubs in the Blue Square Premier receive at the start of each season.

After manager Jim Harvey, who had worked wonders in terms of results given the circumstances, departed just before Christmas, having finally had enough of the mess, the writing was on the wall. The patience of the squad then finally ran out in February 2010, after they had received just one week's wages in the previous four months. They refused to board the team bus to drive them to an away game at Forest Green Rovers and the match was abandoned. Chester City were thrown out of the Blue Square Premier days afterwards and on 10 March 2010 the club was wound up in the High Court owing over £26,000 to HM Customs and Revenue.

Chester's last ever game was against Ebbsfleet United at home, in front of just 450 spectators, on 6 February. They lost 2-1 with Jack Rea getting his name on the scoresheet as the last ever Chester man to find the net for the Blues.

FOOTBALL EXTREME

All games that Chester City played were removed from the league table, creating the strange situation of every club in the division having played at least one 'ghost' game which has been expunged from league records forever. Stephen Vaughan, on the other hand, has remained in the headlines. He was arrested in April 2010 for allegedly assaulting a police officer.

At the time of writing, plans are underway to reform the club in a lower division, hopefully still with the use of the Deva Stadium. Perhaps it won't be long before we see Chester City in the league again. Fans will certainly be hoping their absence doesn't last as long as Accrington Stanley's or Aldershot's.

The Shots folded halfway through the 1991/92 season after a decade of financial crisis brought about by the usual combination of low attendances and lack of on-pitch success, which was coupled with a unambitious board and a 'stick it behind the clock' attitude towards bills.

Teenage millionaire Spencer Trethewy appeared on BBC chat show *Wogan* in 1990 to announce that he was going to buy the club. He invested £200,000 in the club, but it wasn't nearly enough. The club managed to limp on to begin the 1991/92 season but finally admitted defeat in March after a 2-0 loss to Cardiff City. They were bottom of the league at the time.

EXTREME EXPULSION

Supporters rallied to form a new club from the ashes – Aldershot Town – and the new club, still playing at the former club's home of the Recreation Ground, slowly climbed their way up from the Isthmian Division Three to get back into the league again in 2008, 16 years after the original Aldershot had breathed its last. As for Spencer Trethewy, he went to jail for two years for shady financial dealings after his brief stint in Hampshire with the Shots and is now, under the name of Spencer Day, chairman of Combined Counties League side Chertsey Town.

Maidstone United also escaped being in this list by the skin of their teeth. They folded in 1992, just days before the new league season was about to begin. Programmes were printed for their first match of that campaign against Scunthorpe United, which are now collectors' items. A last-ditch attempt to save the team by moving them to the North East and renaming them the Newcastle Browns came to nothing and a reformed club are currently playing in the Ryman League Premier Division – three tiers away from returning to league football. The original club's tenure in the league had lasted just three seasons.

The most famous story remains until last. Accrington Stanley, the butt of many a naff music-hall gag for decades, are currently back in the football league, the reformed club winning promotion in 2006 to League Two an epic 44 years after the original club vanished midway through the season.

The original club should never have been allowed to fold. Stanley were struggling in the late 1950s and were relegated to the Fourth Division in 1960 after a horrendous season in which they'd managed to let in a staggering 123 goals. It was a dramatic slump for a side who only five years earlier had been regularly finishing in the top half of the table in the Third Division North under manager Walter Gailbrath.

Debts mounted, however. A new stand was bought, which then proved to be prohibitively expensive to erect, and in late 1961 Stanley were banned by the league from signing any new players due to debts of over £62,000, over £3,000 of which was owed to other clubs.

As the crisis deepened, a rival stepped in to help. Bob Lord, chairman of neighbouring Burnley, helped Stanley to devise a rescue package – but he then pulled out, stating that the debts were too high. This left Stanley with little option other than to resign from the League altogether. It was 6 March 1962, four days after what would turn out to be Stanley's last ever game – a 2-0 defeat against Crewe Alexandra.

Salvation then seemed to arrive in the form of a

consortium of local business leaders, who stated that they were prepared to invest in order to save the club from extinction. Stanley chairman Sir William Cocker sent another letter to the league, informing them that the club did in fact now have the funds it needed to continue. The league's response, however, was that they had no choice but to accept the club's original resignation letter. Stanley were, in the cruellest and, some would say, most needless of circumstances, out of the league, and a year later, after struggling on in vain in the Lancashire Combination league, they were out of business entirely.

Oxford United took Stanley's place the next season and, as with Chester City and Aldershot more recently, all of the Lancashire club's results from that aborted season were removed from the league tables.

The reformed club didn't play its first game until 1970, and despite being back in the Football League today, the club still suffers from small crowds and a lack of substantial investment. The message appears to be fairly clear. If you have a 'soft spot' for your local lower-league or non-league side, then make sure you pay some money at the turnstile and go and watch them. You may think extinction could never happen to that club near you. But football clubs are businesses like any other, and with the poverty gap between clubs in the top flight and the rest greater than ever, how much longer will it be before the next club is added to this tragic list of extreme failure?

EXTREMELY BRIEF MANAGERIAL CAREERS

How Torquay United hired a new manager – and then fired him again after ten minutes

Will football chairmen never learn? Any football fan with half an ounce of brain will tell you that managers need time in order to produce a side capable of winning things. The two most successful clubs of the last 20 years, Manchester United and Arsenal, have bosses that have been in charge for 24 and 15 years at the time of writing. It's perhaps worth remembering that for the first four years of Sir Alex Ferguson's reign at Old Trafford, the club didn't win a thing. If the board had listened to the 'Fergie Out' chants that were regularly heard at the stadium in the late 1980s, as well as the weekly lambasting of his team in the press, it's hard to imagine that the club would ever have scaled the mighty heights they've reached since then. The board at United were patient, and boy, did it pay dividends.

But football chairmen seldom seem to have this knowledge in mind, often hiring and then firing managers before they even get a chance to buy a player, or in some cases, even move into their office.

Brian Clough famously lasted only 44 days as manager of Leeds United in 1974 before being fired. Perhaps more understandably, Swansea City took less than a week to figure out that appointing a PE teacher with no experience of professional football was a mistake. That's why the door was shown to Kevin Cullis in 1996 after two 4-0 defeats.

DID YOU KNOW?

Tommy Docherty once managed three teams in six weeks. He resigned as Rotherham manager on 6 November 1968 to take over at QPR, but walked out of Loftus Road a month later. He then became manager of Aston Villa on 18 December.

The most extreme short managerial spell, however, goes to Leroy Rosenior. He was appointed to be the new manager of Torquay United in 2007. Leroy had previously been a striker for a variety of London clubs including Fulham, West Ham and Queens Park Rangers and, upon retirement, had a number of management jobs including a four-year spell at Torquay where he took the club to promotion to League One.

However, relegation back to League Two saw Rosenior leave the club by mutual consent and he then took charge of Brentford, a disastrous decision that saw him get fired after a 16-game run without a win.

A press conference was called on 17 May 2007 at Torquay's home, Plainmoor, where it was announced that Rosenior was to be appointed as manager of the Gulls for the second time after the short-term contract of previous manager Keith Curle expired.

Torquay had just been relegated out of the football league and there were rumours circulating that the club could be sold in the near future, but chairman Mike Bateson told reporters he was sure that nothing would happen anytime soon. How wrong he was.

Ten minutes after Rosenior gave his inaugural press conference he was informed that, while the Q and A session had been taking place, Bateson had sold his 50% stake in the club to a new consortium led by local solicitor Chris Boyce. They had their own plans for who they wanted to bring in to the club, and Rosenior was told that he wasn't the man they wanted.

Rosenior told reporters: 'I did the press conference on Thursday, I did all the interviews, and within 10 minutes, Mike [Bateson] called me to let me know he had actually sold the club. So it was something that I knew was going to happen but I didn't think it was going to happen after 10 minutes.'

Failing to take charge of even a single first team game, failing to hold a single training session, failing even to move his things into the club's offices, Rosenior smashed the previous record for shortest managerial reign, held by Dave Bassett for his four days at Crystal Palace in 1984. A notable mention should also go to Keith Mincher, who took charge of one team get together then walked out of Carlisle United after eight days in 1999.

Former Torquay player Paul Buckle was appointed as the new Torquay gaffer and began the road which culminated in the Gulls winning promotion back into the football league two years later.

Rosenoir now works as a pundit for an African pay-per-view football channel and has also since appeared on BBC Radio Five Live. Hopefully he's finding the job security of his new career a little more tenable than his 'stint' in Devon. There's always the chance of a nine minute manager appearing one day, most likely to be courtesy of an impatient rich benefactor to a club but, despite their record of hiring and firing over recent seasons, surely even Manchester City wouldn't consider this?

EXTREME BAD LUCK

When fortune took a short, but highly damaging, holiday for some football clubs

The time-worn aphorism that fortune favours the brave doesn't seem to have much relevance to football. Big or small, deserved or otherwise, every club has had moments in its history that can only begin with the question 'what if...?' What if that vital play off game hadn't been postponed while half of the other team was injured? What if our central midfielder hadn't broken his leg ten games before the end of the season? What if we hadn't sold so-and-so who was 'on the cusp of greatness'?

Trawling through football's archives, though, much as there seems to be a fairly egalitarian spread of misfortune, it certainly seems to have more potency when involving the big sides maybe thanks to no other reason than the inflated egos, rampant posturing and endless post-mortems that, for better or worse, now seem to loom like a storm cloud over 'big time' football.

But they get enough publicity elsewhere. So for perhaps the extreme solution to bad luck, we need to look to the Liverpool suburb of Crosby, and their non-league outfit Marine.

In January 2010, the club were quite rightly feeling cursed. They'd had three of their players sustain serious injuries over the course of the season so far and, on a rare occasion when they were actually winning a game, the floodlights failed when they were 2-1 up and the game was abandoned. The final straw then came when their captain Joe McMahon was in a car crash and sustained whiplash injuries.

Enter Father John Ealey of St Aloysius in Roby, who, at the invitation of manager Kevin Lynch, poured holy water onto the pitch at Rossett Park. It worked a treat. Marine then embarked on a ten-game unbeaten run and rocketed up the table. There were no more injuries, car crashes or broken floodlights. Maybe football is in the lap of the Gods after all.

Even if you're not a believer, Plymouth Argyle must have a strong claim for having gone through the most cursed spell of any club in British history. In the 1920s, promotion wasn't as easy as it is now, with only the top club in the then regional Third Division gaining promotion. Argyle finished second six years running between 1922 and 1927, a quite appalling run of misfortune which, had it happened today, would have seen them promoted with ease.

The outbreak of war is always a curse to a club on a blue streak, and Blackpool fans had more reason than most to hate the Third Reich. When war broke out in 1939 the club was sitting pretty at the top of the First Division, having won all of its first three games. The outbreak of war meant that they remained top for six years until football resumed, but the closest they've ever come to being actual champions after that is finishing second to Manchester United in the 1955/56 season.

In terms of individual players, Michael Owen deserves a mention thanks to his almost surreal catalogue of injuries, which have robbed the player of what should currently be the best years of his career. But the worst luck in Britain, though, has to stand in the form of former Leeds United striker Michael Bridges, who over the course of six years at the club managed an average of only 16.66 appearances per season due to injury. You'd have thought they'd have named the physio room in his honour at least.

DID YOU KNOW?
During a match against Birmingham City in the 1975/76 season, Manchester United goalkeeper Alex Stepney managed to dislocate his jaw while yelling instructions to his defenders. He had to be taken to hospital to have his jaw re-aligned!

It's hard sometimes not to laugh at the sheer outrageousness that bad fortune can inflict, so a final mention must go to hapless Everton. Way back on the final day of the 1904/05 season, they looked to have the championship sewn up. They were beating Arsenal by three goals to one and there were only 12 minutes of the match left to play. The oysters and stout must have already been cracked open in the director's area. Then, an absolute pea-souper of a fog rolled in from the North Sea, leaving the referee with no choice but to abandon the match. The rearranged fixture saw Arsenal win 2-1 and Everton had to make do with a second-place finish; they were just one point short of being champions. There won't be any Everton fans alive now who remember that fateful day, but it could possibly explain why the club have spent so much of the last few years tinkering with a move to a new stadium in Kirkby – it's four miles further inland than Goodison.

EXTREME MIS-MATCH

How Exeter City gave the Brazilian national team a run for their money...

In other walks of life it would seem like an exercise in sadism – or masochism, depending on which side you were on. The chances of Steve Jobs and the team at Apple suddenly deciding to spend a few weeks teaming up with a group of Slovakian radiator salesmen to see if they could produce anything exciting together is, sadly, unlikely to ever happen. Likewise, it would be hard to imagine Barack Obama deciding that the best way to tackle the current economic woes of the United States would be to draft in the skills of a bartender from Sutton Coldfield as his new chief advisor.

Yet, when it comes to football, there still remains the ability, chiefly through the FA Cup, for the mightiest of teams to meet the tiniest of minnows. And what's more, football fans agree almost unanimously that this is a good thing. Football remains perhaps the last workplace where, in given situations, an unemployed postman can be on the same pitch as a man earning £120,000 a week. Anywhere else, this would just be seen as grossly irresponsible, and certainly not in the best interests of the company.

However, the golden age of glorious mis-matches is probably now behind us. Much as the idea of Scarborough playing Chelsea in the FA Cup still holds a huge appeal for real football fans (it happened in 2004 and Chelsea only won 1-0), these are two teams that do at least inhabit two opposite ends of the same footballing universe. For the greatest footballing mis-match of all time involving a British club, we need to travel back to 1914 and a trip to South America undertaken by Exeter City, where they took on the Brazilian national side. It was expected to be an easy win – for Exeter. This was certainly a mis-match, but not in the way you'd think if you saw these two sides on the same fixture list today.

This was officially the very first fixture played by a team representing the Brazilian nation. Wearing yellow for the first time, too, the team was made up of exclusively white players including goalscoring machine Arthur Friedenreich, who, by the end of his career, claimed to have scored a total of 1,329 goals. The idea of this team of amateurs taking on a team of professionals from England was considered to be an incredible step forward for football in Brazil at the time. For the Exeter team, however, this was simply nothing more than the last of eight fixtures they were scheduled to play on a gruelling tour of South America. The players were sick, the backroom staff were exhausted and everybody just wanted to get home to a country which, in just a fortnight's time, would be declaring war on Germany.

The match itself, which took place in Rio on 27 July, was by all accounts a rough game with little to be seen of the silky skills you'd expect from later Brazilian teams. However, two first-half goals, one from Oswaldo Gomes and one from Osman, were enough to make Brazil's very first international game end in a victory over some exhausted Brits who then had a three-week boat journey to make before they could get home.

Even with a colour bar on non-whites and playing against a side from a nation still regarded as being world-beaters at the beautiful game, Brazil had done enough to cause a result that would set the nation on their way to becoming the greatest on earth. And what of Exeter City? Well they ended up with Uri Geller and the late Michael Jackson as celebrity fans and won the Fourth Division championship in 1990. Though, in their defence, picking Pelé for their first eleven was never really an option.

EXTREME SMALLNESS

The most extremely tiny places in the UK to watch senior level football

Teams from outside of the major metropolitan hubs of this island rarely reach the heights of the footballing pyramid. In England, we have to travel back 15 years to find the last time a team from a town rather than a city won the Premiership. Blackburn Rovers achieved their only Premiership triumph to date back in 1995 and are unlikely to be shifting Chelsea, Arsenal and Manchester United from their perch at the top again anytime soon.

But huge admiration most go out to the smaller towns

in the UK which some would say are so small that logic suggests they should barely even be able to field a senior level team at all. Top prize for the most extremely small town to host a professional football club in Britain does not, as many would think, go to Burnley in Lancashire, but actually a club much further north in the town of Dingwall.

DID YOU KNOW?

The lowest ever English Premier League attendance on record came as just 3,039 fans turned out to watch Everton v Wimbledon in January 1993.

With a population of barely 5,000 it's only recently that Dingwall has even had a team in the Scottish league but that team, going under the name of Ross County, are currently soaring. They attract over 3,000 to their home games and, in April 2010, they achieved the greatest result in the club's history, a 2-0 humiliation of the mighty Glasgow Celtic in the Scottish Cup semi-final. All this, as well as being the most geographically extreme team in the whole of Britain, being based further north than any other side.

What exactly is your excuse, Dudley and Rugby, for not even having a league team?

After spending most of their existence in the Highland League, a rare expansion of the Scottish League in 1994 meant that, through a voting system by member clubs, Ross County and fellow Highlands team Inverness Caledonian Thistle were invited to join the league pyramid.

Although the town itself may have only a few thousand inhabitants, Ross County has a catchment area that takes in around 80,000 people. With no real alternatives in the region except Inverness (who have long been unpopular with fans in the lower leagues due to a decision by the boards in the early 1990s to merge Inverness Caledonian and Inverness Thistle to create one 'super' club), Ross County has emerged as the one 'real' club of the Highlands.

Progress up the leagues has been of the slow and steady approach (take note, Gretna fans) and the club now attracts the largest crowds outside of the Scottish Premier League. It may not be long before they get their chance to compete with the giants of Glasgow for, having already beaten Celtic in the 2010 Scottish Cup semi-final, a promotion push is a realistic target for the next couple of years.

It's an incredible achievement for a team playing in a

town whose entire population could fit into Wembley Stadium eighteen times over. Whether their current success is a flash in the pan, or whether they're here to stay, depends very much on the random nature of the SPL's approach to stadium criteria. The current capacity of their ground, Victoria Park, is 6,800, with much of the stadium being given over to terracing. The SPL's demand for all clubs in their division to have all–seater stadiums, a rule brought out in the aftermath of the Hillsborough disaster in 1989, means that if Ross County are forced to leave their ground, their supporters will no doubt face some epic treks to wherever their 'home' games could end up taking place.

The SPL's stance that it is safe to stand for spectators when Ross County play Dundee in Division One, but suddenly not safe when they face Falkirk in the SPL, is something of a bizarre one. If Ross County can upgrade their ground, or find suitable new accommodation when the time comes to mix with the big boys, then there's a real possibility that the first genuine footballing force to come from the Highlands could be upon us. If not, then one of Britain's most extreme football teams may never get the chance to show us just what the most northerly town in Britain to host a senior level team can do.

EXTREMELY BAD MATCHES

0-0 draws are one thing, but how about a goalless snooze-fest where neither team had a single shot?

Call it nerves, call it cynical tactics, call it just plain inability, but it's sadly true that for every barnstorming cup final or promotion decider, there are at least 20 absolute stinkers. Sometimes you can understand the reasons. Managers are hardly going to ask their team to take risks, or bravely attempt some Dutch-style 'total football' when all they have to do to win promotion (and in doing so earn enough money to see the club's financial situation improve from ruinous to merely troubling) is scrape a point against Gillingham. There are few players out there who are going to start attempting to dribble the ball past five different opposition players when all they have to do is cling on to a one-goal lead for another eight minutes in order to win the FA Cup.

But sometimes, it can all just go a bit too far. There have been some rotten FA Cup finals over the last few years, the 2008 final between Cardiff City and Portsmouth being a particularly dire example of what can happen when two clubs, in a extremely rare Wembley appearance, know they can't take many risks as they're chances of appearing in a cup final again anytime soon are rather slim.

The Liverpool v Manchester United final in 1996 was another quite staggering anti-climax – a 90-minute exercise in fear from two deadly rival clubs who just knew there was too much at stake to really play with confidence. As is the way in those types of games, the match was decided in United's favour by a goalkeeping error by David James, which allowed Eric Cantona to score the only goal of a dismal match.

The winning entry for the most extreme bad match in British history, however, is one that gave us a combination of cynicism, back rubbing and total disregard for the hard-earned cash handed over at the turnstiles, which took place back in 1898 between Stoke City and Burnley.

In these early days, there was a huge amount of tinkering with issues such as how promotion and relegation between divisions could be decided. For this season, a mini-league was formed of four teams – Stoke City, Newcastle United, Burnley and Blackburn Rovers – to see who would go up and down between the first and second flight.

There was a tiny flaw in the plan, however. Previous results meant that by the time Burnley and Stoke played each other at the Victoria Ground on the final day of the mini-league, a scenario had emerged where both Stoke and Burnley knew that a goalless draw would be enough to keep City in the top flight and to get the Clarets promoted from Division Two. The pioneering Corinthian spirit of the game, supposedly ubiquitous in those far-off days, was certainly nowhere to be seen over the next 90 minutes during what has to be the worst match in British football history.

Both teams knew that they had to do precisely nothing in order to keep their status. So that's exactly what happened. Not a single player had a shot on goal throughout the entire game. Burnley keeper Jack Hillman didn't touch the ball all afternoon, and the main source of entertainment came from the fans.

To voice their discontent at the way the non-game was progressing, supporters kept on keeping the ball every time the players kicked it into the crowd – which must have been many times on that day.

Fans kept the ball hidden under their coats, one ball ended up on the roof of the main stand, and one got thrown into the River Trent behind the ground! At least five balls were used that afternoon. A policeman was deployed to run the touchline to try and retrieve them but the hopeless copper, whose eye was obviously a little too concentrated on the ball, collided with the linesman, sending both of them onto the floor in a heap.

Needless to say, the mini-league idea was scraped after this goalless farce and the system of automatic promotion and relegation we know today was put in place the following season. It's not recorded how many fans asked for their money back, and it's a safe bet to say that street football games were popular in the following few weeks in the Stoke-on-Trent area. After all, a lot of the balls in use had just come directly from the pitch of a top flight game!

EXTREME SEXISM

Can men beat women at football – even with one arm tied behind their backs?

Were the 'good old days' of football really all that? You don't have to go too far into football's back catalogue to find examples of racism and sexism that would quite frankly boggle the mind of even the most unenlightened of 21st-century fans. Racist abuse aimed at non-white players was common until the early 1990s and there is perhaps no sadder picture to sum up 1980s British football than that of Liverpool's John Barnes, the most talented British player of the decade, kicking away a banana that had been thrown at him by a 'fan'.

Prior to that, black footballers often acquired a strange sort of novelty status, with noted bigot Ron Atkinson dubbing the black signings in his 1970s West Brom side 'The Three Degrees'. Truly painful stuff. As for sexism, the women's game may be thriving in nations like the USA and South America today, to say nothing of the steady progress of the England women's team under manager Hope Powell, but it wasn't that long ago that the notion of women playing the game at all brought as much mirth as it did abuse from the menfolk.

Back in 1917, the debate was already raging as to whether the women's teams that did exist at that time had any right to even consider the possibility that they may one day be able to compete with male footballers on a level playing field.

To test this theory, a game took place in Reading between a team of women and a team of men. Somewhat surprisingly, the game was allowed to go ahead despite a Football Association ruling dating back nearly 20 years in which it was clearly stated that matches should not be permitted between men and 'lady teams'.

Somehow, however, this exhibition match – between Canadian male soldiers and British women – took place on a dismal Wednesday afternoon at the home of Reading FC, Elm Park. The oddest part of this most odd of matches was that the men had taken it upon themselves to decide that they should play with one hand behind their backs. Whether this was to prove their superiority, even with a handicap like this, or whether the decision was made in order to 'give the ladies a chance', the result was certainly an interesting one – for the women's team.

Reports tell us that the women won by eight goals to five. The Canadian soldiers, stationed in the UK for the duration of the First World War, claimed afterwards that they hadn't really been trying all that hard and that a lot of them were still recovering from injuries sustained in fighting. But we've all heard excuses like that. Goals from Miss Bentley, Miss Small, Miss Wragg and Miss Barrell (who bagged herself a hat-trick) were enough to prove, to at least some degree, that women were far from useless at this supposed gentlemen's sport.

And it was only three years later that the first international women's game took place – starring Dick Kerr's famed women-only factory team from Preston, who beat France 2-0 in front of 25,000 fans at Deepdale, home of Preston North End.

Dick Kerr's side also drew the largest ever attendance to date for a women's game in Britain, when an incredible

53,000 turned out to watch them beat a St Helens ladies team that same year. Incredibly, the FA then banned women from playing football altogether, believing that the popularity of all-female teams was threatening the male game. It was as late as 1971 before the FA officially recognised women's football, six years after Dick Kerr's side, later renamed Preston Ladies FC, had disbanded despite highly successful tours of the USA.

The England women's team must yearn for crowds of even half that size today. Women's football may be more high-profile than it has ever been in this country (though that's not saying much compared to the men's game) but back in 1917, sexist as it was, that extreme football match in Reading may well have done something to convince more enlightened members of the football establishment that, in their own dated parlance, 'these girls can play a bit'.

EXTREME REFEREEING

Don't slag off the referee next time he makes a mistake. At least he didn't score for the opposition…

We've all seen the men in black make howling errors – the response to which from the crowd, since time immemorial, has been to question the individual's eyesight, sexuality and propensity to engage in acts of onarism. But perhaps after reading about this particular moment of extreme refereeing, you may feel compelled to ease off the next bungling ref who appears to have a rabid dislike for your team.

DID YOU KNOW?

Wendy Toms became the first woman to referee a senior match in England on 31 August 1996 when she took charge of the Conference match between Woking and Telford United. Woking's Andy Ellis was the first player to be booked at that level by a woman after he was given a yellow card for dissent.

One of the longest journeys in English football was the trip between Plymouth Argyle in Devon and ex-League team Barrow in Cumbria. On 9 November 1968, there were only a couple of hardcore fans who had made the epic journey north. And they were going to be made to wish they hadn't bothered, as they were about to witness the only recorded example of a referee scoring the winning goal.

With the game goalless after 77 wretched minutes, Plymouth manager Billy Bingham (who would later go on to manage the Northern Ireland national team) must have already had half his mind on the gruelling coach journey home that lay ahead for him and his team. Then Barrow player George McClean attempted a shot that appeared to be heading straight into the arms of Argyle keeper Pat Dunne. But the referee, a certain Mr Ivan Robinson, failed to get out of the way of what should have been a routine collection for the keeper. Hitting Robinson on the inside of his left foot, the result was a mean-looking back-heel as the deflected ball spun past a bemused Dunne and into the net.

Incredibly, FA rules state that if the ball rebounds off the referee or an assistant referee when they are on the field of play, then the ball is deemed to be still in play and the game must continue with no stoppages. So the goal had to stand. Barrow claimed the goal for George McClean, but everybody in the ground that day knew that it was the man in black who had actually scored the winner for the Cumbrian side. Robinson apologised, but that was hardly any use consolation Bingham and his Plymouth players. It turned out to be one of Barrow's best ever seasons in their league history, as they finished eighth in Division Three, their best ever finish and a club record that stands to this day. They lost their league status in 1972, to be replaced by Hereford United, and the team these days plays in the Unibond League.

As for Mr Robinson, why he wasn't offered a player's contract by gaffer Colin Appleton and the directors at Holker Park that day has never been fully explained.

DID YOU KNOW?

The first penalty kick was awarded to Wolverhampton Wanderers during their match against Accrington Stanley on 14 September 1891. The kick was taken (and scored) by John Heath and Wolves won the match 5-0.

EXTREME MAGNANIMITY

How a Premiership team offered to replay a game they won – despite doing nothing wrong

If you're looking for gallantry, valour and magnanimity in sport, well, the yachting books are probably on the next shelf. Even in lower-league and non-league football, while the cliché of 'real' teams playing football for love and nothing more does exist, one of the worst fights I ever saw on the pitch happened during a supposedly meaningless friendly between two teams in a village league in South Cheshire. So, for extreme generosity and a quite staggering example of altruism and fair play, it's with a decent pinch of disbelief that we travel to Arsenal's former home of Highbury for an FA Cup sixth round clash against Sheffield United in 1999.

With the game poised at one goal apiece in the 76th minute, United player Lee Morris collapsed with suspected cramp. An informal agreement that had slowly been taking hold in the football around the world since the early 1980s suggested that the protocol for a when an injured player needs treatment should be as follows: the ball should be kicked out of play while the physio examines the prostrate player. Then, when the referee signals that the match can continue, play should restart with the ball being given back to the team whose player had been injured.

However, it seemed nobody had told Nigerian international Kanu this. Team-mate Ray Parlour had sportingly thrown the ball towards the United keeper, and Kanu, in his debut appearance for Arsenal, decided to chase after it. Sprinting forward, he passed the ball to an unmarked Marc Overmars, who simply tapped the ball into the net. Arsenal were in front – and Sheffield United were furious.

It's still unclear as to whether Kanu hadn't spotted that Morris needed treatment, or whether he just simply wasn't aware of the gentlemen's agreement with regard to injured players – but that seems unlikely, given the amount of international football he would have played where this arrangement would also have been standard practice.

Either way, despite Arsenal having technically done nothing wrong, manager Arsène Wenger announced at the final whistle that his side would be prepared to replay the game as a gesture of goodwill to Sheffield United, who had come so close to earning a lucrative replay, and their supporters.

It was a totally unprecedented situation. FIFA were called in to confirm whether Wenger's suggestion was actually going to be viable. The governing body announced that the replayed game should go ahead, but that a percentage of the gate takings should go to charity and that both clubs must agree beforehand that the result of the next game should stand, no matter how contentious any goals scored may be.

The next game, again played at Highbury (much to the chagrin of some United supporters who felt the game should be taking place in Yorkshire) resulted in the same score, 1-0. Arsenal were through to the next round of the FA Cup.

Sheffield United boss Steve Bruce and Arsène Wenger both claimed to be happy with the situation – but it would have been hard for anyone at Sheffield United to be too disappointed by their unexpected replay. Under the rules of the game, Aresnal had done nothing wrong. So Wenger's offer to replay such a crucial game as an FA Cup tie that his team had already won surely must go down as the most gallant in recent British football history.

It didn't do them any good in the long run, though. They lost in the semi-finals to eventual winners Manchester United after a replay. The first game, unlike their extreme clash with Sheffield United, did actually end in a draw.

EXTREMELY SMALL LEAGUE

The tiny British island where every team has a 50% chance of winning the league

Having to compete against at least three dozen other sides for the chance of winning a league title is more than a little onerous. The margins of failure are, of course, absurdly high and there are clubs such as Crewe Alexandra who have never once been champions of a division in their entire history.

So how about a division where your side's chance of finishing as top dogs is precisely 50%, every single season? This is the extreme reality of life on the Isles of

Scilly, where a grand total of two teams compete for the championship every year.

With a population of only 2,000 and with many people of playing age leaving for the mainland due to a lack of jobs that aren't related to tourism, it's something of a miracle that this tiny group of islands (of which only five are inhabited) located off the coast of Cornwall can sustain a 'league' at all. It also goes some way to explaining why some of the team members are well over 60 years of age.

Yet the Woolpack Wanderers (who play in claret-coloured shirts) and the Garrison Gunners (who play in yellow) turn out regardless to play 13 matches a season – plus two cup competitions in which both clubs are, of course, always guaranteed a place in the final. It's a bizarre situation for the islands, which back in the 1920s actually had a whopping total of five teams, one each for the inhabited islands of St Mary's, Bryher, Tresco, St Martins and St Agnes.

It's the football version of having a needle stuck in a record. The same players dutifully turn out each week; some have done so for many decades. Crowds are small (usually no more than a dozen) and, thanks to another eccentricity, there is no chance of one side dominating the 'league' for too long. This is because, before the season begins, both clubs pick from all the available players on the islands. This means that almost everybody has played for both sides in the course of their career. The Gunners have won more titles since the league began in 1962, but matches are often high-scoring affairs with title races frequently going down to the last day of the season.

It should therefore come as no surprise to learn that, with a league this small, both sides share the same ground. Garrison Field has been guaranteed to be the location of a title victory parade every season since time immemorial. It's perhaps worth a visit for any success-starved supporter from the mainland who would like to witness a footballing high on the last day of the season as their own team staggers home to another 14th-place finish. It's also a good opportunity to start singing 'Can we play you every week?' – though I've got a hunch the lads from the Wanderers and the Gunners may just have heard that one before.

EXTREME GOALS BY INANIMATE OBJECTS

If you ever have the moronic urge to throw something onto the pitch, please read this first…

There have long been apocryphal stories swirling around Sunday league football about an occasion where a dog invaded the pitch and prodded the ball over the line. Sadly, there isn't enough evidence in the UK for any of these stories to be confirmed. But there have been plenty of other occasions where inanimate objects have definitely played a crucial role in the outcome of a match.

Take the case of a coffee cup, which was a surprise

influence in a match between Derby County and Nottingham Forest in 2004. Barry Roche, in goal for Forest, had to think quickly as a back pass from a team-mate somehow managed to hit a coffee cup that was lying on the pitch and went horribly astray. His botched clearance went straight to Derby's Paul Peschisolido, who hammered home what would turn out to be the second in a 4-2 thumping of their rivals.

Back in 1996, Blackburn Rovers goalkeeper Tim Flowers was comprehensively outwitted by a divot in a Premier League match against Liverpool. Deploying the oft-used goalkeeper's tactic of kicking holes in the turf so he could get a bit more welly on his placed goal kicks, the hacked greenery then wreaked a terrible revenge on him when a poor shot from Stan Collymore hit one of the divots, bounced over Flowers, and trickled into the goal.

The king of the inanimate goalscorers, though, has to be the beach ball which scored the only goal of a Sunderland victory over Liverpool at the Stadium of Light in 2010. The ball became a hero for Sunderland supporters and fans of the faintly ridiculous alike, and although its location today is unknown there was a strident campaign in the *Sun* for England boss Fabio Capello to pick the beach ball over hapless striker Emile Heskey in the next international fixture – when you compared the goals/minutes played ratio of the two, the beach ball came out firmly in the lead.

This bizarre event happened in the sixth minute of the game, when Sunderland's Darren Bent struck a shot which looked to be heading straight into the hands of Liverpool keeper Pepe Reina. But that was before a huge beach ball lying on the pitch made a memorable interjection – with the football deflecting off it and into the net. Worse still, footage on YouTube clearly showed that it was a young Liverpool fan who had chucked the ball onto the pitch in the first place.

'It was just one of those things', claimed Liverpool manager Rafa Benitez after the game. Looking at the Laws of the Game, however, it is clear that should the football hit an 'outside agent', whether it be a beach ball, a bucket or a bacon sandwich, the referee must stop the game and restart play with a dropped ball. Neither manager seemed to be aware of this, though Mike Jones, the man in black for this bizarre incident, was widely criticised by fellow referees for making such a basic error. The Premier League ruled out any possibility of the match being replayed, though Jones didn't escape entirely unpunished. The next week, he wasn't chosen to referee any of the

Premiership fixtures. Instead of reffing in the big time, Jones was seen at London Road officiating Peterborough v Scunthrope.

EXTREME CUP SHOCK ENGLAND

How Altrincham became the very last side to travel to a top-flight club and knock them out

Nothing quite captures the imagination of the British public, as far as sport is concerned, than a good old-fashioned cup shock. It's one of the few times that a tiny club can expect to receive national attention, plus of course the obligatory acres of space on the back pages with photos showing the victorious team spraying champagne around in their dressing room while in a state of semi–undress.

Everybody has their opinion as to the most extreme

166

cup shock in the English FA Cup to date. Walsall's shock defeat of one of the greatest ever Arsenal sides at Fellows Park in 1933, by two goals to nil, is certainly up there with the best of them. In more recent times, strong contenders are Sutton United, who beat then top flight Coventry City in 1989 (a mere two years after the Sky Blues had actually lifted the trophy themselves) and Wrexham, who having finished the previous season bottom of the entire league, famously beat reigning league champions Arsenal 2-1 thanks to an incredible free kick by veteran Mickey Thomas in 1992. And there surely can't be a football fan alive who hasn't marvelled at archive footage of Ronnie Radford getting mobbed by fans in snorkel parkas after belting in a goal from 35 yards out which set Hereford United on their way to beating Newcastle United in a third-round replay in 1972.

DID YOU KNOW?

Bury hold the record for the biggest FA Cup final win – they beat Derby County 6-0 in the 1903 final.

FOOTBALL EXTREME

My choice for the most extreme cup shock is, in my opinion, the most shockingly overlooked cup upset in recent history. It's notable as, despite the tie happening a quarter of a century ago, it remains the last time that a non-league club has gone to the ground of a top-flight side and beaten them. There are no YouTube clips of the game, and it seldom gets mentioned in newspaper round-ups of greatest-ever cup shocks.

But what happened on a wet evening in Birmingham in 1986 signifies a classic FA Cup moment which looks less and less likely to be repeated in the near future. These days, if you want a cup shock, you'd better hope that your team gets a home draw because (unless you're an Altrincham fan) you're unlikely to have much of a memory of your own lower-league or non-league club beating a top-flight side on their own turf.

For it was Altrincham FC, then playing in the Alliance Premier League (one level below the Football League) who, on 14 January 1986, travelled to St Andrews, home of Birmingham City, to record an outstanding 2-1 victory. City were, it should be noted, having a dreadful season. Manager Ron Saunders actually went as far as to say that he expected Altrincham to get a result, such was the paucity of his own malfunctioning side. He quit the club two days after this incredible cup tie took place.

Altrincham were at that point one of the best sides outside of the football league and had regularly beaten league teams in the early rounds of the FA Cup during the late 1970s and early '80s, whilst also earning commendable draws against Everton and Tottenham Hotspur.

Tragically for them, the structure of things at the time still didn't allow automatic promotion into the Football League for the top sides in what is now the Blue Square Premier. To Altrincham's eternal frustration, they had to make do with regular cup shocks and live in hope that a club lower down the league chain would go bankrupt, thereby giving them a chance to fill the space.

Future Arsenal and England keeper David Seaman was in goal for Birmingham City that day, and he saw his side go one goal up with a strike from Bob Hopkins, before Kevin Ellis gave the Moss Lane non-leaguers a deserved equaliser.

City's night was only to get worse. In the second half, Hopkins scored a tragic own goal when a back pass to Seaman missed the keeper completely and rolled into the net.

Sadly for Altrincham, despite being only the second non-league side in history to beat a top-flight club on their own patch, they couldn't find enough to make it over the next hurdle, as York City won 2-0 at Bootham Crescent in the fourth round two weeks later. Altrincham's glorious cup run was over, and in the long term, so were their chances of gaining entry to the league.

The FA's decision to open up promotion for non-league sides to enter the realms of league football in 1987 coincided with Altrincham falling from their perch as the top side outside of the league. Today, they continue to play in the Blue Square Premier, but have not mounted a promotion challenge for many years and are considered by many to be one of the weaker teams in the division, partly as a result of the club's players still being part-time.

Perhaps the time will come when they can finally make a push for a league place, but in the meantime, they still hold the record of being the architects of one of the most extreme cup shocks of all time − and they've given fans of other Midlands clubs over 20 years of laughs, too.

EXTREMELY LARGE CROWDS

How nearly 300,000 people turned up at the same ground in the space of a week for just two games

Unless you're a fan of Wigan Athletic, capacity crowds at Premiership games are nothing unusual these days. Old Trafford's capacity may still be an impressive 75,000 but in these days of heightened safety concerns, all-seater stadiums and extended corporate facilities, it's no longer necessary for many more than 40,000 people to show up to most matches in order for the commentators to start gushing about a 'heaving crowd'.

Frankly, the number of people turning up to top-

171

flight matches in Britain today are pathetic compared to years gone by. At full capacity, the new Wembley stadium can squeeze in 90,000 for major cup finals, but this is still paltry compared to the most extreme high attendances this country has ever witnessed. What's more, the two highest attendances in British history both occurred at the same ground, and in the space of just one week. Wembley may claim a reported 200,000 for the chaotic first FA Cup final held there in 1923, but this is purely an estimate. For the official record, we must head to Glasgow and one of the oldest international stadiums left in existence.

Hampden Park is the home of the Scottish national team, and also of Queens Park FC, the last amateur side still competing in the Scottish league. Eerily, Queens Park's home games attract gates of only a few hundred, in what even by today's standards is still a large stadium capable of holding up to 52,500.

Opened on 31 October 1903 with a capacity of 40,000, Hampden grew to become the largest stadium on earth until the Maracanã in Brazil was completed in 1950. At its peak, 150,000 could get in and it was during this period that the two record attendances were set.

A vast bowl situated in the area of Mount Florida in Glasgow, the stadium had just one seated main stand

and one tiny stand perched on top of the opposite side. The rest of the ground was a vast bowl of open terracing stretching back for what seemed like miles. Primitive and uncomfortable the arena certainly was for most spectators. Until the early 1980s, the terracing was made up entirely of ash and timber rather than concrete.

The stadium was staggering in its dimensions even when empty. But when the place was full, it was the noise of the home crowd, known as the 'Hampden Roar', that gave the ground its legendary reputation as one of the most intimidating places on earth for opposition players. The phrase 'Hampden Roar' was coined by a journalist after Alex Cheyne scored for Scotland in the last minute in a game at the ground in 1929 and the crowd roared non-stop all the way to the final whistle.

For the next few years, the crowds only continued to get bigger. The first record came on April 17th 1937 when an absolutely awesome 149,415 people paid to get in to watch Scotland play an international fixture against England. Despite the hostile Hampden Roar, England were one up at the half-time break – but the crowd must surely have played their part in the second half as Scotland fought back to win 3-1. Officials in attendance claimed afterwards that the crowd was closer to 160,000 thanks to supporters breaking the turnstiles in order to cram themselves in.

Incredibly, only a week later, the ground was packed to the rafters again for the Scottish Cup Final between Celtic and Aberdeen. Willie Buchan scored a second-half winner for the Glasgow side in a 2-1 victory. The crowd of 147,365 is the all-time record for a British domestic fixture, and with the largest stadium in Britain now holding a mere 90,000 it looks like being a record that will stand forever.

Redevelopment, and a slow reduction in the capacity of Hampden, began in the late 1940s and continued bit by bit until the ground was made all-seater. The old main stand – the last surviving part of the original ground – was eventually replaced by a new structure in the 1990s. Hampden will never see crowds of such an incredible size again, but the Roar is still alive and well, albeit without quite such an extreme number of people to contribute as there was in that incredible week in 1937.

EXTREMELY COLD WEATHER

How the elements have conspired to wreck British football over the decades

Spectators have it far too easy these days. Roofs on stands are the norm, seats are plentiful and if they end up watching their team let in their third goal of the first half, fans of the top sides can always retire to the concourse underneath the stand for a beer and a hot dog.

As for the players, they may still have to face the elements, but the combination of global warming, undersoil heating, power showers in dressing rooms and the acceptance of the practice of donning gloves and cycling shorts whilst on the pitch means that the prospect of the British weather decimating a team whilst they're actually still playing is now a very remote one indeed.

Predictably, you have to go way back to football's early years to find the very harshest of conditions. A match between Wrexham and Lincoln City in Division Three North in 1927, for example, was abandoned when four – count them, *four* – Lincoln players collapsed because of the extreme cold and driving rain. The most worrying part of this statistic is that the game took place in April!

Occasionally, conditions have been so extreme that players have actually died. In 1896, a certain James Logan of Loughborough Town died on the pitch from pneumonia and in 1909 James Main of Hibernian sustained fatal injuries on a frozen pitch whilst playing against Partick Thistle. A heavy challenge with a Thistle player saw Main sustain stomach injuries which would eventually go on to kill him four days later.

Extreme cold weather can lead to matches being postponed multiple times – and the record for the number of times a 'match called off' sign has been placed by the turnstiles is an incredible 33. In the bitter winter of 1963 a Scottish Cup game between Aldrie and Stranraer only took place at the 34th time of asking – with Aldrie eventually running out 3-0 winners.

DID YOU KNOW?
The record number of matches called off in a single day came during the Second World War. Only two of the 56 wartime matches in England and Wales on 3 February 1940 actually took place.

The nationwide freeze of 1963 prompted more extreme behaviour – this time further south. With snow drifts of up to 25 feet and temperatures regularly dropping down to -20 degrees The Shay, home of Halifax Town, was opened to the public as an ice rink while Yorkshire neighbours Barnsley were able to play only two games between 21 December and 12 March.

Further south at Carrow Road, home of Norwich City, the club resorted to using flame throwers in an attempt to thaw out the pitch – an attempt that ended in dismal failure as the ground simply refroze as quickly as they could set fire to it. Meanwhile, Chelsea attempted to use a tar burner and Leicester City experimented with a hot air tent. Nothing was a match for the greatest white-out in British football history –

and it was late March before the fixture list could be fully resumed.

Perhaps this shocking winter was the reason why, just as the snow was thawing out around Britain, a truly horrendous moment in world history occurred. Was it the escalation of the Vietnam War? Or perhaps it was publication of the Beeching Report, which would lead to half of the UK rail network being scrapped? Well, yes it was all of these things, but none were surely as bad as – in what can only be assumed to be a collective spell of insanity on behalf of the British public after enduring the worst winter of the century – the fact that 'Summer Holiday' by Cliff Richard went straight to number one.

EXTREMELY BAD FOOTBALL SONGS

Like a convincing Nigerian internet scam, or a nattily-attired British builder, good football records are a rare thing indeed. New Order's 'World in Motion', released for the Italia 1990 World Cup campaign, stands (apart from John Barnes's ill-advised attempt at rapping) as pretty much the single glorious exception. It must have been good, as the record placed higher in the German charts than their national team's own attempt.

The litany of abysmal football records is a vast one, though, and far too big to document in anything near its full glory here. Many of the records are a curious amalgam of exaggeration, bad synths and communal singing that makes most school assemblies sound like the Three Tenors.

Notable mentions must go to an early 1980s effort by the players of East Stirling FC. The chorus had the memorable refrain of 'We are the Shire, we are the Shire. We're only going to go higher and higher'. In 2007, the club finished bottom of the entire Scottish Football League for the fifth consecutive season.

The big clubs aren't immune to the equation of 'bad record equals bad result' either. Liverpool FC recorded the quite exceptionally horrible (even in this tough field) number entitled the 'Anfield Rap' in 1988, before their FA Cup final with Wimbledon. It was John Barnes's first recorded attempt at rapping – though in the company of John Aldridge and Jan Mølby, he sounded like a prototype Mos Def. But despite the team's musical efforts, Liverpool lost the final 1-0 in one of the biggest Cup upsets of all time.

Individual players are rarely brave enough to give singing a go, but Kevin Keegan unwisely decided to have a bash at a pop career, releasing 'Head over Heels' in 1979. Even back then, good taste in music prevailed and the single stalled at number 31 in the charts.

Gazza, as in so many things, was another exception, having hits with a cover of 'Fog on the Tyne' and 'Geordie Boys (Gazza Rap)' both of which, thanks to YouTube, we can still enjoy today. In the latter video especially, Paul looks like a tour rep for a Club 18–30 holiday in Corfu. Heady days indeed at the height of Gazza-mania, the memory of which is enough for football fans of a certain age either to pine for or wince at the thought of inflatable bananas on terraces and the sight of England actually coming close to winning something.

In more recent times, Andy Cole released a cover of the Gap Band's 'Outstanding' whilst still a Manchester United player in 1999. Chris Lowe of the Pet Shop Boys actually wrote the tune, which is probably something to remind yourself of the next time he and Neil Tennant announce one of their pretentious 'concept' projects based on ancient Russian films.

But one thing all these disasters did have, however misplaced it may have been, was a sense of fun. So the winner of the most extremely bad football song is one that is not just rooted in fatalism, it's also one that is unbelievably depressing to listen to. Step forward Del Amitri, and their anthem for Scotland's 1998 World Cup finals appearance in France.

Entitled 'Don't Come Home Too Soon', the message is a doomed one from the start. Scotland have never managed to progress beyond the first round of the World Cup tournament in their entire history, and this was hardly the song to get the fans and players hyped up before taking on the likes of Brazil – to whom they, inevitably, lost in the opening match of the tournament. The song is so utterly miserable in tone, so clearly the most risible opposite of a rousing terrace anthem, that you could imagine it being played to get the spirits up in the dressing room before the game about as much as you could imagine the present Scotland squad winning the World Cup itself. Which is sort of appropriate, really.

EXTREME FATNESS

The tubbiest footballers ever seen

Football fans don't seem to have much of a sense of irony. I've lost count of the amount of times I've seen 18-stone men staggering up from their creaking seats at games to shout 'Who ate all the pies?' at a player who eats in a week what said supporter would probably consider to be a 'light bite' before breakfast.

A choice few footballers, however, really were unapologetically huge. First in line is the rather chubby form of Thomas Brolin. He looked good playing for Sweden in the European Championships in 1994, but by the time he arrived in England to play for Leeds he looked like he'd exchanged the herring and rye bread of his home country for a diet of pie and chips. Fans at Elland Road couldn't believe he was the same player and it wasn't long before he was offloaded to Crystal Palace where, if anything, he got even bigger.

Legendary Everton goalkeeper of the 1980s, Neville Southall, was well-known for carrying more than a little extra baggage around his middle, though it didn't seem to stop him from being one of the greatest keepers of his generation for both the Toffees and for Wales. His last club was Bradford City, and by the time he got between the sticks at Valley Parade, he pretty much seemed to fill up the entire goal – again, no bad thing as long as he wasn't required to jump, dive or bend over too many times to pick the ball out of the net.

On the other side of Merseyside in the same era resided the shirt-stretching frame of Liverpool's great Dane, Jan Mølby. One of the most sublime midfielders ever to grace English football, his genius was such that he spent the latter part of his career barely moving at all except to spray out inch-perfect, defence-piercing passes. His incredible footballing eye meant that he pretty much single-handedly won the 1992 FA Cup final for Liverpool – without ever leaving the centre circle of the pitch.

And then there was Newcastle United's Mick Quinn, who waddled around the pitch to become a fans' favourite during their lean years in the early 1990s. There was nothing lean about Quinn, however, who looked like the kind of player who'd be constantly looking for an excuse to nip off the pitch for a pasty without anyone noticing. When questioned about his ability, Mick commented that he was 'the fastest player you'll ever see over one yard'. Magpies fans didn't seem to mind, serenading him with the chant 'He's big, he's round, he's worth a million pound'. Which was quite a lot of money back then. Enough to get around 4,265 Big Macs, if my calculations are correct.

The all-time legend, however, weighed in at a quite extraordinary 24 stone by the end of his playing career. William 'Fatty' Foulkes holds the record for being the biggest player who has ever puffed his way onto a British football pitch. A goalkeeper for Sheffield United and Chelsea at the turn of the 20th century, Foulkes was no gentle giant. Possessed of a terrifying temper, he would simply walk off the pitch if he thought that his defenders weren't pulling their – ahem – weight. Opposition players who barged into him would end up being thrown into the goal net, and even referees incurred the giant's wrath.

In 1902, he had to be restrained by FA officials from

ripping a door off its hinges to attack a cowering ref – who had hidden in a broom cupboard to prevent a mauling after Foulkes had decided that an equalising goal for the opposition shouldn't have been allowed.

Foulkes died in 1916 and it's believed that one of the causes of his death was the fact that he had caught pneumonia after playing football for too long on the beach at Blackpool. Whether he was actually playing football or simply spending his time at the seaside eating as much candy floss as he could get his hands on is something that scholars have yet to reach agreement on.

EXTREME PERSONAL FAVOURITE

The author's most extreme footballing moment

I was always jealous of the lads in my year at school who took no interest in football. OK, so I thought it was a little strange how a 14-year-old male couldn't understand the thrill of the parent-free bus rides, illicit cigarettes, smuggled cider cans and loud swearing that made up a Saturday afternoon watching Wrexham FC in my neck of the woods, but at least they weren't in a position where they needed to care about their own abilities on the pitch.

Unlike me. Being a football obsessive, but yet also

stinking out the field every time I put on my muddy Golas, was a constant source of irritation and frustration. My only excuse was that I had terrible eyesight, which neither glasses nor contacts ever seemed to improve. So my tactic was to become a goalkeeper. Not the greatest of positions for the visually challenged, I'll admit, but I figured it was either that or become a referee – where I may have been able to, ahem, 'see' the point in the howls of abuse that would no doubt have come from spectators questioning my ability to see ten yards in front of me, but would probably have ended up with serious psychological issues when questions regarding my propensity to onanism arose.

I wanted to be Bruce Grobbelear; the eccentric clown who could also produce match-winning saves. Alas, I was a total non-starter when it came to the latter part of that job description, but I was fantastic at fumbling crosses, letting shots roll under me and grinning sheepishly after my latest gaffe – to the increasing animosity of my team-mates.

However, there was one small, and quite extreme, piece of our school's football history which I was destined to be a part of – notably, the most extreme amount of blood ever seen on a school football pitch in the Chester area to this day.

It was a Sunday morning. I was 14 years old and, out

of sheer desperation on behalf of our school PE teacher, I had been drafted into the 'C' team for an inter-school tournament, the prestige of which was so questionable that I'm surprised the FA didn't step in after the event and decide to use the competition as a replacement for the Group Cup.

I was keen to impress, but sadly the night before I'd been even keener to show off my ability to drink the contents of my Dad's drinks cabinet in a corn field near our house with some defiantly football-hating friends.

My hangover the next morning made it feel like I was being punched repeatedly in the forehead by a staple gun. Turning up on the pitch feeling rather queasy, already in my kit (unwashed, naturally) it wasn't long before the opposing team, who looked frankly world-class from where I was standing, had me picking the ball out of the net for the second time.

As another attack from these apparent Cheshire-based Brazilians surged forward, I pulled off my own Gordon Banks moment. A shot was fired towards the goal, and it looked to be heading hard and low into the bottom corner. I managed to propel myself to the left and dived – straight into the goalpost. The ball bounced off my stomach and away to safety. My already delicate head, however, had just been given the most almighty of blows. I thought I might just about survive – as long as I didn't have to move for the next three or four days.

Picking myself up, I noticed one of my defenders looking towards me and suddenly turning all pale. I raised my gloved hand to my head and it was only then that I realised there was a veritable Niagara of blood spurting out of my forehead. Looking back towards the goal, I saw a now heavily-bloodied nail sticking out of the post. I'd dived not only into a goalpost but also into a quite shockingly dangerous piece of DIY.

Everything after that happened in a blur. The defender fell forward, hitting the ground in a dead faint. The entire two teams rushed towards him. It only emerged some time later that he was afraid of blood and had promptly fainted at the sight of the cascades of claret that were churning out of my skull.

I was whisked off to hospital in some kind dad's car and ended up receiving 12 stitches in the gash in my forehead. It was the last game I ever played for my school. The reports from my classmates on Monday morning revealed that the area by the goalpost had to be covered with sand in order for the game to continue without any more fainting taking place. Somehow, I felt slightly proud. I'd created the most blood seen on a school field since the early days of the Eton wall game.

It may not have been pretty, and it may have extended

that staple gun feeling from mere hours on a Sunday morning to a period of time that seemed to last around a fortnight, *après* stitches, but nonetheless my small place in the footballing history of our school was established. I may have been utterly useless, but I'd literally shed blood for that team. And I'd created perhaps the only incidence in history of a football player fainting at the sight of his goalkeeper's face. Extreme? Yes. Painful? Yes. Was it worth it? Of course not. I never could get the blood out of my goalie jersey.